I0220620

Robert Cooper Seaton, Robert Cooper Seaton

Six letters from the colonies

Robert Cooper Seaton, Robert Cooper Seaton

Six letters from the colonies

ISBN/EAN: 9783337109431

Printed in Europe, USA, Canada, Australia, Japan

Cover: Foto ©ninafisch / pixelio.de

More available books at **www.hansebooks.com**

[PRINTED FOR PRIVATE CIRCULATION.]

SIX LETTERS FROM THE COLONIES.

By R. C. SEATON.

HULL : WILDRIDGE & CO.

MDCCCLXXXVI.

PREFACE.

WAS absent from England eleven months, from November, 1884, to October, 1885. The first three of these Letters are reprinted, with slight alterations, from the *Eastern Morning News*. The last three were written after my return to England. As I have not cared to keep up the fiction of having written them from Australia, they may contain some references to events subsequent to my return. It is often objected, and truly enough, that travellers, who spend only so short a time as I have in fresh countries, are not justified in expressing deliberate opinions about them ; but this does not apply where a writer gives his impressions as such, and not as matured opinions, or where he expresses the opinions of other people who, by long residence or otherwise in a particular country, have had every opportunity of forming them. I think it will not be found that I have offended in this particular.

LONDON,
    October, 1886.

Digitized by the Internet Archive
in 2007 with funding from
Microsoft Corporation

http://www.archive.org/details/sixlettersfromco00seatiala

CONTENTS.

I

The Voyage of the Hampshire.

VOYAGE to Australia has in these days become so ordinary an affair that it may seem to require an apology to attempt to describe one, but a voyage in a sailing ship is so different from that in a steamer that it may interest some people. It is, as a rule, only those who go abroad for their health who prefer a sailing ship, on account of the great length of the voyage, in allusion to which steam people call sailing ships "wind jammers," while the sailors retort on steamers by dubbing them "iron tanks" and "old coffins." There is no doubt that the picturesqueness of a sea voyage is quite destroyed by a steamer. There are no, or very few, regular sailors on board; so much of the work is now done by steam. There are no "chanties" or sailors' songs, which help the work to go easily. In a steamer there is no interest in noting the course—they go straight on, and the distance covered does not vary, or only slightly, from day to day. The movement of a sailing ship through the water at 12 knots per hour is quite exhilarating; the ship hurries on by "leaps and bounds." Contrast with this the labouring plunges of a screw-steamer at the same rate. In short, romance is perishing from the sea with the universal invasion of steam. Could the poet have thus written of the Pirate—

> " O'er the glad waters of the deep blue sea,
> Our thoughts as boundless, and our souls as free,"

if the Pirate was master of a steamer? I think not. However, I do not deny that a steamer has many and great advantages over a ship. The chief advantage, and the only one to which I need allude, is the prosaic but not unimportant one of better food, and this with many people would decide in favour of a steamer. Perhaps we were exceptionally unfortunate in this respect. The Hampshire is a barque of 1,100 tons, and belonging to Captain Hosack, of Liverpool. She is most commodious ; the cabins are much larger than is usual in a vessel of this size. Mine was not a large one, but it measured 8ft. by 10ft. 6in. There is, too, a poop deck 70ft. long, which is scarcely ever touched, even by a heavy sea. When people are constantly in each other's society for so long they gradually throw off many of the artificial restraints of society, and exhibit themselves as they would in their own homes. The result is curious. A constant process of natural selection goes on, by which like seeks like, and the estimation in which a particular person is held by his fellow-passengers is often very different at the close of the voyage from what it was at the beginning. Taking all things into consideration, however, I think the saloon passengers on the Hampshire must be considered to have borne the ordeal very well. We were 24 in number—rather too many for comfort—all (with two exceptions) young men, going out to the colonies for various reasons—some for health, some for business. The two exceptions were a Canon of the Church of England and his wife, and another gentleman who was travelling with his nephew. The Canoness was the only lady on board, the result of which probably was that, though the civilising influence imparted by the presence of ladies was lost, yet many jealousies, that might have been thereby occasioned, were avoided.

The Hampshire left the East India Dock early on Thursday morning, the 27th November, commanded by Captain John Mathias. She was towed as far as Beachy Head, but laid up at Deal during the night. At St. Alban's Head we parted with the pilot. On the Monday we left the Lizard behind. The next ten days were the most unpleasant of the whole voyage. We were tossed about in the Bay of Biscay, making scarcely any progress. One day we even made 16 miles leeway. It was, perhaps, well that this happened so early on, as all seasickness was thus comfortably got over. Since that time the weather may be shortly dismissed. Captain Mathias, the officers, and crew all declare they have never had so fine a voyage to Australia.

B

For days and days the sea was only slightly ruffled, and hardly
any motion could be felt. Of course, one result has been that
we had a long passage. We were exactly 100 days from dock
to dock, or 96 days from the Lizard to Cape Otway. The
longest run in the 24 hours was in the Southern Ocean—254
knots. During the latter part of the voyage we usually made
over 200. During the week ending February 15th the distance
covered was 1,408 knots; that ending February 22nd only 945
knots, the wind having fallen light; the following week,
however, it was 1,503 knots. About 16th December Madeira
was passed about 30 miles on our left-hand. On the 26th we
passed San Antonio, the most westerly of the Cape Verde
Islands, at a distance of about 40 miles. The line was crossed
on the 7th January, about 5-30 p.m. All through the tropics
the heat was not so great as I had anticipated. It was never
more than 87 degs. in the shade and 105 degs. in the sun.
The temperature remained about the same night and day. The
sea was about 6 degs. cooler than the air. The daily routine
was about somewhat as follows :—About six the hose was used
for cleaning the deck, and then such of the passengers as chose
came on deck and submitted themselves to it—others meantime
pumping for them. Those who had the hose thereby acquired
a right to porridge, which was distributed about a quarter to
seven, but, when the weather was colder, even the porridge was
not sufficient attraction to keep up the number of " hosees."
Breakfast was at 8-45, lunch at 1, dinner at 6. The captain,

chief officer, and doctor occupied the chief seats at the tables. They changed their seats from time to time to prevent jealousy, as the captain's company was much in request. Indeed, any inconveniences we had to put up with were so much alleviated by the kindness and consideration of Captain Mathias, that he will ever be gratefully remembered by the passengers on this voyage. The address of thanks to him at the end of the voyage was no mere lip-service, but the genuine expression of our sincerest thanks. On all occasions he managed to combine the courtesy of a gentleman with the frankness of a sailor. After passing the equator we had to sail very much to the west, to catch the south-east trades, and were within 100 miles of the coast of Brazil. On the 60th day out the meridian of Greenwich was crossed in lat. 38 degs. south. "The meridian of the Cape of Good Hope," says the captain's log, "was crossed on the 65th day out, in lat. 35½ degs. south, and the longitude was run down in the parallel of 42 degs. south. Light winds stuck to the barque persistently, and as an illustration of the tedious weather, it may be mentioned that not a topgallant sail was taken in from Biscay to St. Paul's, and the average running in crossing the Southern Ocean was only 161 miles per day." The last land sighted was the Island of Trinidad—an uninhabited rock—in lat. 20°45' south, long. 29°48' west. This was on the 16th January, and for seven "solid" weeks from then we were out of sight of land. This time was redeemed from monotony by tournaments of chess and whist, which filled up the evenings. There were frequent small quarrels, with reconciliations more or less sincere, which also afforded distraction. After one the captain let off a rocket, also one of Holmes's patent " flare-ups." This is a contrivance for saving life during the dark. It consists of a box filled with potassium, which is pierced at both ends and thrown into the sea fastened to a life-buoy. In contact with the water the metal ignites, and for about half-an-hour sheds a radiance for a long way. It is visible for miles off. If a man falls overboard he knows then where to look out for the life-buoy.

The Canon was an adept at shorthand, and a class was formed on board of 12 of the saloon passengers, who prosecuted it most vigorously, and really made much progress. An examination was held at the end of the course of lessons, and prizes awarded. Several entertainments—musical and dramatic—were given, nearly all of which proved successful, the very causes of failure on land being often at sea the cause of success. The prompter was, I remember, on one occasion much more audible than the actor. Another time the stage (the main deck) was flooded with sea water, which increased rather than diminished with every roll. A chorus of youths and maidens endeavouring to sing and keep their balance is amusing if not æsthetic. Everything, in fact, suffers a " sea change," if not into something " rich and strange," often into something expensive. The first time a passenger ventures on the forecastle or up the rigging—the peculiar realms of the sailor—Jack chalks him, which means that he must pay his footing, by sending a bottle of whisky for'ard. It is seldom that a stranger long escapes "spotting" under these circumstances. As a curiosity I may mention that one passenger paid 8s. for a few things being washed ; this was at the moderate price of 6d. each article, no matter whether it was a collar or a shirt. I should strongly advise anyone going a long voyage to take a spirit lamp, as it is often difficult to get hot water unless the thirst of the cook is constantly allayed. Deck shoes are very convenient, more especially in the tropics, where one leads a lotus-eating existence. This is the most delightful part of the voyage in my opinion, though some prefer the more bracing air of the Southern Ocean. Without being malicious, however, it is difficult not to fancy that the pleasure of finding midsummer weather in January is heightened by the contrast with London fogs and frost, which we know those at home are suffering from. The greatest resource of all is reading, and some of us get through a good deal of it, but it is too tempting, and often interferes with taking regular exercise, which, though irksome, is almost essential to good health at sea.

Christmas Day seemed strange enough. The orthodox fare—turkey and plum-pudding—were on the table, but ice would have been an agreeable addition. The toasts drunk were "The Queen," "The Captain," and "Absent Friends." The next day, as we had then been a month at sea, the sailors "buried the dead horse." As they receive a month's wages in advance, they do not begin to earn anything until they have been a month at sea. During this period they are said to be " working off the dead horse." A barrel covered with matting formed the body, and appendages for the requisite number of legs and the tail were put on. The animal was then dragged round the deck to the accompaniment of a melancholy song— the refrain of which is " poor old horse." The horse is next put up for sale, and on the present occasion was knocked down to one of the saloon passengers for 16s. The money was not really paid, but a collection was made which came to more than the sum bid. Next, amid the lamentations of the sailors and the glare of blue lights, the animal was hoisted up to the main-yard with a sailor on its back, who, dexterously disengaging himself, let the beast fall with a dull thud into the water. The sea was so calm that some apprehension was expressed lest the carcass should be seen the next morning not far to leeward, but this anti-climax was averted. We have all read of the coming on board of Neptune at the time of crossing the line, but on our voyage no notice was taken of it, the reason being, as was supposed, that the sailors were dissatisfied with the result of the sale of the dead horse. Well, though it might have been amusing, it was doubtless more their loss than ours, because when the thing is analysed, all sailors' doings fundamentally resolve themselves into an appeal for subscriptions from good-natured passengers. About 15th January we crossed the sun, which for a short time was vertical at noon. Peter Schlemihl could then have walked about without detection, for no one had a shadow.

On our journey we met several ships and steamers, and as the captain never missed an opportunity of signalling, the course of our voyage was known from various quarters. First, the number of the Hampshire, JNBV, is displayed by the flags, each flag representing a letter. A complete code of arbitrary signals is in use, by which almost any intelligence can be interchanged. We then told the port we sailed from, London, and our destination, Melbourne. From one barque, the County of Anglesea, on her way from Cardiff to Rangoon, which we fell in with early on the voyage, the captain came on board the Hampshire to lunch, and afterwards several of our passengers returned the visit. One of them brought back a small cur, which made the fourth dog on board—rather too many, as they were always in the way. Their number was soon reduced 50 per cent. One day what was known as the "sailor's dog" mysteriously disappeared. Some thought it had been thrown overboard, but it probably fell over accidentally, as the dog was universally held to be the least objectionable. Another, the strange dog, had to be poisoned. On the 10th January we met a German ship bound for Barbadoes from Buenos Ayres. Here an opportunity for sending letters was gratefully embraced. The captain promised to hand them over to the British Consul at Barbadoes. One day, during a calm, the boats were lowered, and several of us rowed about to look at the Hampshire from a little distance, while some bathed in a tropical sea. There was no danger of sharks, which keep away when several bathe together, or even one, if he splashes about enough. The boatswain caught a turtle, from which we had some capital soup. Turtles are very tenacious of life. A knife was thrust into its throat, and its jugular vein severed, but if it had not been cut up soon after it would have lived many hours. Indeed, the heart alone kept beating long after it was severed from the body.

I must say we were badly treated by the "monsters of the deep." They never came out when wanted. We all expected to catch a shark some day, but only once was one even seen, and then it was some distance off, with its knife-like fin just showing above the water. It was Sunday, too, when no fishing was allowed—a fact of which he was evidently aware. These fellows are proverbially stupid, and will go at a bait again and again, even though they must know it to be a lure. Only once, too, did we catch an albatross, *the* bird of the Southern Ocean. That was by a line baited with a small piece of pork. This was fastened to a round ring of iron, in which the hooked beak of the bird caught, and so it was dragged on board. The captain knocked it on the head, and it was then cut up. It measured 13 feet across the wings, but many are larger than this. The beak was about 6 inches long, curved, and of great power. Sailors have no "ancient mariner" sentiment as to killing the albatross—in fact, it would be misplaced. The captain told us of a case he knew of where a man had fallen overboard, when the albatrosses swooped down upon him, and pecked out his eyes and brains. The sailors begged the captain to shoot him and so end his sufferings. The quills of the albatross make excellent pipe stems, and the skin of the webbed feet is used for tobacco pouches. But the chief thing about the bird is, of course, the snowy down on the breast, of which ladies' muffs are made. The Zoological Society in Regent's Park offer a reward of £100 for a live albatross or black cockatoo, but it has never been earned, though the attempt to carry them to England has often been made, for the albatross cannot live through the tropics.

During the last fortnight of the voyage the weather became very cold for the latitude we were in. The point reached furthest south was 42° 42' which is about the same as the north of Spain, but the thermometer was 49 degrees all day. It is, however, well known that for various reasons the same latitude is much colder south of the equator. On the night of Monday, the 2nd of March, a beautiful lunar rainbow, extending right across the sky, was seen. This is not a common sight. By this time the benefits of the voyage were visible in the faces of all the passengers. If it had not been for some shortcomings in the provisions there would have been no drawback. Cape Otway was sighted on the morning of Saturday, the 7th March. At 4-30 p.m. we were off Port Philip Roads, and here the pilot came on board. He brought papers, and the first news we read

c

was that of subscriptions for a statue to General Gordon, of whose
death we were thus informed; the second news was the de-
spatch of troops from Sydney to the Soudan, of which everybody was then talking. At 10-30 p.m. the Hampshire was
anchored off Williamstown, but could not come alongside Sandridge Pier, till Monday morning. It was rather hard getting
up on a Saturday night, as all were anxious to see their letters.
Many of us went to Melbourne on the Sunday, but in most
cases returned to the ship to sleep, as the luggage could not be
landed till Monday. On that day a general dispersion took
place, and many who will probably never see each other again
will have their voyage on the Hampshire to look back upon
with pleasure.

II.

Melbourne.

HEN I arrived in Melbourne early in March, everybody was enthusiastic in praise of the New South Wales Government, who had just despatched their contingent to the Soudan. Gradually this feeling subsided, and it was afterwards said to be doubtful whether the Victorian Government would renew their offer later on. The truth is the Victorians are *plus royalistes que le roi.* Indeed I cannot help thinking they would feel much less respect for the " British Constitution " if they had a nearer view of some of the proceedings at Westminster. But they are human and can scarcely submit with patience to the repeated snubs they have had from the Home Government. The inconceivable bungling about New Guinea especially rankles in their breasts. No one is now so unpopular here as Mr. Gladstone and Lord Derby. Moreover, as a late Minister in South Australia said to me—Why should we send out our tradesmen, our artisans, our clerks, as volunteers, while you send out regular soldiers? We deplete the colony for what is in reality only a handful of men, while it means much to us. If we wish to assist the mother country we can do it better by taking care of our own defences, and by subscribing money, if necessary, to send to England. But this view, of course, leaves out of sight the immense moral effect which has, in fact, been produced by this display of attachment to the mother country. Such things will do more to bring about Imperial federation than any number of articles in newspapers and reviews discussing the merits of various schemes. If the true spirit is there—the desire for federation—it will put itself into practice in some form or other. The preliminary step is federation among the colonies. This is at present much hindered by their mutual jealousies. "The proper way," said to me a prominent statesman here who has been twice a Minister of the Crown, "is for England to take the initiative. Let her send out some leading man who would not be regarded as the representative of a party—such as Lord Dufferin—and let him make proposals to the various colonies in which they might acquiesce, without one seeming to lead the others." Anyhow here, "as at home" (as England is always called), there is a widespread notion that federation in some form is a necessity for the future, if England is to continue to hold her own by the side of such immense states as Russia and the United States. Providence seems now to be on the side of the "big nations." I am confident that even now, people in England fail to realise the importance of these homes beyond the sea. They enjoy a lovely climate, have boundless capacities for expansion, and are inhabited by Englishmen who differ from ourselves only in the fact that they live at a distance. With the present means of communication, Melbourne is now as near to London as the North of Scotland was to the South of England less than a century ago. People look, perhaps, at the present population of Victoria, which is rather under a million ; and then, observing that it is about the same as that of Liverpool and Manchester together, they infer that it is of no greater importance. There could not be a greater mistake. It is a commonplace to say that their importance is in the future, yet even commonplaces sometimes need repeating. There is no reason why, within the memory of men now living, this colony should not be as populous as England is now. At lunch, some few weeks ago—I remember it was at Dr. Bromby's, the much-respected late head master of the Church of England Grammar School—a clergyman narrated some of his experiences while travelling in England a few years back :—" I was at the house of a Yorkshire squire, who was speaking of Australia, and said ' Ah ! we used to have a few Australian sovereigns here, but now we see very few.' I requested those present to examine the sovereigns they had about them. If you find an ' M ' under the Queen's head, it was coined at Melbourne ; if an 'S,' at Sydney. Singularly enough nearly all the sovereigns they produced had the ' M ' or the 'S.' I was satisfied. It was a dangerous *coup*, but perfectly successful, and gave the company a much greater idea of the importance of Australia than anything I could say." In rapidity and at the same time solidity, of growth there is no city of modern days, I believe, to be placed beside Melbourne. Fifty years ago it did not exist. Now with the suburbs the population is 300,000, and in such a liberal manner have the streets and roads been laid out, that on the present area there is at least room for a million. Since 1842 Melbourne has had municipal institutions. In 1851, Victoria was separated from New South Wales, with Melbourne for the seat of government. Such rapid increase has been equalled only in America, but there is nothing American about Melbourne. Many years ago there did come here a few Americans of "advanced ideas," among others the notorious George Francis Train, who bequeathed his "damages" against the British Government—5,000,000 dols. for his arrest in Cork harbour—to the Irish Republic. The legacy and the legatee have proved equally unsubstantial. But these men have now died out, or become respectable citizens. The colonials may be said to resemble the Americans only in one point, in their aptitude for business. Some people have come out here in the expectation of "taking in" the guileless colonist, but the biter has been bit. I have heard of one manufacturer of pills who soon found out his mistake.

In fact, in face of the nonsense that is sometimes talked to encourage those who fail in England to come here to make their fortunes, it seems to me they are far more likely to lose what money they have. As a rule the same qualities of mind and character that bring a man success in England will make him successful here, and for certain people it is better to stay in England. The class that really suffer in Melbourne is that comprising the man of good education, who has perhaps taken his degree at one of our Universities, but who has not any fitness for any particular calling. Numbers of this class are, I am told, in poverty, if not actual want. There is here not the same demand for "culture." There is no outlet for purely literary capacities. The life that is led here, and which will be led for some time yet, is a somewhat hard and fast life, and it is most difficult even for one who desires ease to find it in this feverish atmosphere. The country has scarcely yet settled down. Among the population there is little beauty of face or grace of movement. The first settlers were, as a rule, rough people who had to make their living, and little time to think of anything beyond, but we are indebted to them, for they are everywhere the necessary pioneers of civilisation—the mass whose dead bodies form a bridge for their more fortunate successors. Then the gold discoveries brought out a lower class. However, the second generation is a great improvement on the first, and, no doubt, the usual rule of amelioration of type will make itself felt in due course. In what I have just been saying I speak in the most general manner. There are many exceptions, of course, and brilliant ones. Now to return to Melbourne itself. The streets are very broad, usually 99 ft., and long and straight. One I know of is 100 yards broad. Some are planted with trees, while in the streets where there are shops, verandahs are almost universal along the pavement. The gutters are very wide—sometimes 5 feet or 6 feet, which is necessary to carry off the large amount of water coming down when it rains. At such times the mud is almost impassable. Melbourne proper is situated in the centre, and stands to the rest of the city somewhat as the City of London does to the various vestries. In Melbourne, however, each of the suburbs —15 in number—has a Mayor, Corporation, and Town Clerk of its own. Any municipality with a revenue of £25,000 or above, is styled a "city." There is, however, no body here like the Metropolitan Board of Works, consequently no united system of drainage and other works in which the whole community is interested. This is a great defect, and the want of some central authority is much felt. Each municipality manages its own district only. I remember, on landing the first time at Sandridge Pier, some of us drove from there into Melbourne. Someone complaining of the badness of the road to the driver, " Yes," he said pathetically, " they spend all the money in drainage."

In public buildings Melbourne can compare well with any other city of its size. The Public Library, the Law Courts, the Town Hall, the Post Office, the Exhibition building, are all architectural ornaments. In the streets there is a want of regularity in the size of the houses, which will be corrected in the course of time, and which is incidental to all new cities where people cannot at first afford to erect lofty structures. Most of the city is on the north side of the Yarra, which winds very much and empties itself into Hobson's Bay, about six miles from Melbourne. The intercolonial and local steamers start from wharves on the river, and passengers by them have, therefore, to endure the bad smells which always prevail. The Thames is bad enough sometimes, but the Yarra can only be compared to the Clyde at Glasgow. A large piece of the river will be cut off by a canal now in course of construction. Hobson's Bay is the north-eastern part of Port Philip Harbour, a noble expanse of water of 800 square miles, with a narrow entrance at the " Heads." There are sharks in it, so that bathing is carried on in parts that are fenced off. There used to be a reward offered by the Government for every shark-skin above 2ft. long. There is a tale of an old loafer round the Harbour called " Paddy Lynch," who having caught a shark of 1ft. 11 in., stretched its skin the required inch. He is now commonly accosted by the question " Who stretched the shark ?" The Public Library is probably one of the largest and completest of its kind to be found anywhere. It now contains about 120,000 volumes, and is rapidly increasing. A new wing is being built to make more room. The trustees have acted with a view to acquiring books of real worth, and no book is selected unless it has made its reputation. Consequently the amount of fiction

D

is small. George Eliot's novels have only just been admitted. The library is not supported by a local rate, but by the Government. The same is the case with all the public libraries throughout the country. However small a township is, you will probably find a public library and a mechanics' institution. In the same building with the library are the Picture Gallery and the Museum. In the former are Miss Thompson's "Quatre Bras," Long's "Esther," and "A Question of Propriety," the latter bought off the easel, besides other good paintings. In the vestibule are plaster casts of some of the aborigines, labelled, "Martha, aged 14;" "Thames, aged 50;" and so on. They are all remarkably ugly, but vary in degree, some being actually repulsive. There are now only a few hundred natives in the whole of Victoria, and they are miserable creatures, not to be compared, for instance, with those in the north-west, where in some places the average height of the natives is 6ft. The library is open daily (except Sunday) from 10 a.m. to 10 p.m. Some time ago the trustees did open the Library and Picture Gallery on the Sunday, but after five Sundays Parliament sat, and the Sabbatarians then immediately passed a vote prohibiting it, although the measure had been very popular. In fact, nothing is open on Sundays. Public-houses are shut, except to that remarkable animal—the *bonâ fide* traveller. A few weeks ago there was a deputation to the Premier, urging him to stop all Sunday trains. This was supported by some ministers who are themselves in the habit of using trains on Sunday, but they did not find the time ripe for such a change.

I had an interesting conversation with the learned and accomplished Town Clerk of Melbourne (Mr. Fitzgibbon) upon the condition of the legal profession here. The two branches, barristers and solicitors, are not amalgamated, but the tendency, as in England, is in that direction. Indeed, in the last session of Parliament a bill to amalgamate them, after passing the Legislative Assembly, was only lost by one vote in the Upper House. Still, even in places where a fusion has taken place, as in Tasmania, I found that, in fact, they are kept distinct, that is to say one man will devote himself to speaking in court, another to office-work. Barristers here have a distinct grievance against the Inns of Court at home. Here an English barrister can be at once called to the Victorian Bar merely by being introduced, whereas in England a Victorian barrister has to keep terms and pass an examination. Formerly he was in no better position than any other student, but by the exertions of Mr. Webb, Q.C., of Melbourne, the time of probation has been reduced from three years to one year for colonial barristers, and the examination has, I believe, been diminished also. There is a Chief Justice (at present absent on leave) and four puisne judges. Lately a paper controversy has been raging between one of the judges and the Bishop. The judge wrote a pamphlet, entitled " Religion without Superstition "—a crude *réchauffé* of the usual sceptical arguments which have been propounded a thousand times before and infinitely better expressed. The Bishop has not found it difficult to reply, but at best this contest between two dignitaries is an unseemly spectacle. Meanwhile the newspapers sarcastically ask how it is that the judges, who are said to be so overworked, have time for such amusements. Religious feeling runs high in Melbourne. The Presbyterian assembly has recently deposed Mr. Strong, the minister of the Scotch church, on account of the breadth of his doctrines. Mr. Strong has been publicly invited by the Unitarian minister to join their communion. In the State schools there is no religious instruction except at extra times, and by express desire. This is due to the action of the Catholics, who naturally object to their children being taught the Bible by Protestants. About Melbourne there is nothing provincial, and, although in point of size far inferior to London or Paris it is almost as cosmopolitan. At night, Bourke-street is as crowded as the Strand or Regent-street. The chief hotels are Menzies's, Scott's, the Oriental, and the Grand. The two first are at the business end of the town, the west end, and they charge about 12s. per day. The Oriental is at the east end of Collins-street, exactly opposite the Melbourne club. The charge there is 10s. per day, and at present it is extremely well managed by the proprietor in person. The only objection is that it is much frequented by betting-men, whose shop talk is, I think, more wearisome and less instructive than that of any other persons. The Adelaide Jockey Club have just been holding their annual meeting at Melbourne on account of an attempt by the South Australian Legislature to abolish betting! On the whole the prices of things in Melbourne may be said to be about the same as in London. Some things are much dearer, and not so good, as for instance, cloth clothes, boots and shoes. Again, house-rent is excessive. I can give two examples—one, a cottage of one story and four rooms, which lets for 22s. 6d. per week; another, what is called a seven-roomed house, but it really has only four rooms, the other three being merely of the size of dressing-rooms ; this is in not at all a fashionable part, and the rent was lately £98. It has now been raised to £108. Every house, however, has a bath-room, and the old houses in which there is no bath have to be fitted with that convenience before they can be let. On the other hand, food, especially meat, is much cheaper, but the meat is not so good as at home, at least in my opinion, but I can scarcely expect this opinion to be accepted without objection. A fish called "garfish" is about the best fish here. It is something like a whiting, but has more taste. Another fish called "trevalli" is not particularly good. There is no sole or turbot or salmon. The colonial wine is, upon the whole, very good and wholesome, and is much drunk. At Geelong lately the heroic measure of destroying the vines has been taken to prevent the spread of phylloxera. There are several good clubs in Melbourne—the principal are the Australian at the west end of the town, and the Melbourne at the east end of Collins-street. On the introduction of a member (approved by the committee), strangers are admitted as honorary members for a month : then for the second month they pay £1, or £6 for six months; but strangers cannot be taken in casually by a member as is the case in many London clubs. Most of the clubs have bed-rooms attached, which are much used by travellers in the colonies. They are, therefore, not merely more comfortable, but usually cheaper than hotels, because meals are paid for as taken, while at nearly all hotels the American system of so much a day prevails.

One day I accompanied a friend to the University to be present at the "annual commencement," when the degrees are conferred. The "commencement" here occurs about the middle of the term. With us at Cambridge it is at the end. The ceremony took place in the "Wilson Hall," which is used as a Senate House, and for other public functions in connection with the University. The ceremony itself was almost identical with that at one of our Universities, and it was similarly interrupted by noisy Undergraduates, whose humour consisted in rendering the proceedings inaudible without contributing anything amusing of their own. One lady who took a degree was much cheered. The Bishop of Melbourne (Dr. Moorhouse) is the Chancellor, and delivered an address to the "fractious children," and he then called on the Governor of the colony, who with Lady Loch was present, for a speech on the subject then foremost in every one's mind—"Our Defences." This seemed rather strange at a peaceful academical performance, but the Governor acquitted himself in a truly diplomatic style, by telling us nothing we did not know before. On another day

I was shown over part of the University by a young gentleman who had taken his degree in law on the previous occasion. There are at present two colleges—Trinity and Ormond—at each of which about 35 Undergraduates are in residence, while there are about the same number at each non-resident. The bulk of the students, however, are unattached. There are 350 altogether, and their number is annually increasing. There is no University discipline outside of the Colleges, and in them the students take their meals together. The sitting-rooms are separate from the bedrooms, and more resemble studies at a public school than rooms at a University, being usually shared between two and furnished by the College. There are no fellowships at the University. At Sydney University on the other hand four fellowships of £400 a year each have been recently given to the University for the encouragement of scientific research—a munificent gift which should lead to much.

To strangers, the climate of Melbourne is trying at first. Suddenly, in the summer the wind will turn to the north, and in a short time the thermometer registers 100 degs. in the shade. The heat and dust are then almost insupportable. The dust rises like a cloud obscuring even the opposite side of the street. Then the wind will as suddenly veer to the south. In an hour the temperature falls 40 or 50 degs., and the air is cleared by a "southerly buster." In the winter the north wind is a cold wind. In spite of the climate, the Botanical Gardens are an admirable specimen of what may be effected by the skill of man. These gardens are on the south side of the river Yarra. On a hill in the centre of them is built the Government House. There are seen many varieties of trees and plants all carefully labelled. The fern tree bower is very ingenious. You see here the elk or staghorn fern, which grows as a parasite on the palm or the petosperum of New Zealand. The grass is kept beautifully fresh and green, and is a favourite resort. I have no further room to continue this letter, but, in my next, hope to say something of the government and the aspect of politics in Victoria.

III.

Victoria.

—>—<—

HE Government of Victoria is nearly a pure democracy. Both Houses are elected by the people, the Legislative Council as well as the Legislative Assembly. To vote for the former a slight property qualification is necessary, viz., £10 freehold, or £25 leasehold. The Assembly is practically elected by universal manhood suffrage, the only restriction being that a voter must have resided twelve months in the colony prior to the 1st January or 1st July in any year. Of course, there is a smouldering agitation for female suffrage, but it has not yet attained the dimensions of the similar agitation in England.

It is to me unintelligible how it is that so many people can be enthusiastic about the prospects of Democracy. As Sir James Stephen says, " We may be drifting down the stream, but that is no reason we should sing Hallelujah." There is no

E

magic in the word. It is simply a form of government, just as monarchy or aristocracy are forms of government. Nor is it a new form of government. It has been tried over and over again, more than 2000 years ago, nor has it ever been a particularly successful or a long-continued form. People often talk as if liberty were more attainable under a Democracy than under any other government. Now, putting aside the question whether liberty is good or bad—for it is entirely a question of time, place, and circumstance—the opinion is unfounded, because the tyranny of a majority is just as galling, and usually less intelligent, than other tyrannies. It has rather cynically been said that governments are of two kinds—bamboo and bamboozle. A Democracy combines these two kinds. When political power is so minutely divided as it is among the voters of England, say, it is not worth having ; and power, as a rule, resides in the hands of demagogues, instead of the hands of statesmen.

In Victoria, there is government by party, but there are no real lines of demarcation between them, and it is now merely a struggle for office between the ins and outs. Each party must be prepared with a programme to interest the masses, and to be able to go to the electors with a list of measures to be passed. If a measure is bad, the Government may be turned out. But the ministers are saddled with no responsibility in consequence. They simply wait their turn till the other side makes a mistake. This course has led to legislation which unduly interferes with liberty. There is now before Parliament a new Licensing Bill, the principle of which is Local Option. It is also intended to put down barmaids. Those who at present exist are to be allowed to remain, 346 in number, but no fresh ones are to come forward. The publicans are ranged on one side, some religious bodies on the other. Each side interpret facts in their own way. But every one knows that the fate of the bill will depend on the strength of the parties in the House, and not on argument. Again, the eight hours movement many years ago became law in Victoria. On the 21st of April in each year its anniversary is celebrated with a procession and flags and banners. This year the Governor took part in it, which was thought to be rather undignified on his part. It is a Socialistic measure, which reduces the good workman to the level of the ordinary one. All members of the Assembly receive £300 a year. Hence there are many professed politicians whose chief object appears to be to keep their seat. Lately there was an attempt in the House to vote a pension to a member whose circumstances had been reduced, but the proposal was defeated. Perhaps the time is not quite ripe for that yet. The present Ministry is the result of a coalition between Mr. Service and Mr. Berry. The former was at one time a schoolmaster up the country, but by his talents and energy has raised himself to the position of Premier. Mr. Berry is a well-known Radical politician. It is about six years ago since, in one day, he dismissed the greater number of the Civil servants in consequence of a disagreement between the two Houses. Most of them had to be quickly restored to their places, but public confidence was so much shaken by this arbitrary act that a large amount of capital was transferred to New South Wales—five or six millions, I believe—and even yet the country has not recovered from the shock. This period is known as the Berry-blight. The present Ministry seems likely to continue in power so long as they can provide sufficient sensational legislation.

In Victoria the railways all now belong to the State, and are well managed, but to stations beyond the suburban lines return tickets are not issued except on Saturdays, and except to such places as have a competing steam service, such as Warrnambool or Belfast. The speed is not high, and to our notions there are very few trains, but probably enough for the present traffic. Whenever the inhabitants of any particular district think they would like a railway, they get their representative to vote for it, and if he can persuade a sufficient number of other representatives to vote for it, the railway is made. For some time past the people of the small town of Buninyong thought they would like a line from Ballarat, from which it is distant seven miles. As it is not really required, in consequence of a good service of public conveyances between the two places, they did not succeed for some time. At length, during the last session, their repre- sentative managed to get 35 others to vote for it, and the line is now to be made. Each of these 35 may in their turn require the vote of the member for Buninyong on some similar occasion. But the actual management of the railways and of the Civil Service has been put beyond the reach of political influence by the appointment of Railway and Civil Service Commissioners, who are permanent officials. When a line is to be made the Railway Commissioners go over the ground and fix the spots for stations &c. Every porter has to pass on examination before he can be appointed. There are only first and second classes. On the suburban lines the first class are about as good as our second. As a fact, a number of second class carriages sent out from England are here used as first, the words "second class" being ingeniously concealed by a narrow strip of wood. Members of Parliament have a free pass over all lines. In Victoria the gauge is 5ft. 3in. In New South Wales it is the same as ours, viz., 4ft. 8½in. Consequently travellers between Melbourne and Sydney have to change trains at the border.

In Victoria there is intense opposition to Free Trade. The people would rather make bad boots and shoes for themselves than import cheap and good ones from England. Of course I use Free Trade in the sense of the opposite of protection of native industries. Advocates of Protection appear to me to confound the end with the means, as if manufacturers existed for their own sake and not in order to produce. I have seen the commercial competition between various countries compared with a horse race. Just as some horses are handicapped, so customs duties must be levied on the productions of certain countries to give the others a fair chance! The comparison would be relevant if the object of a handicap were that the best horse should win, but the race itself is the object. Bastiat has reduced this view of commerce to an absurdity in his famous petition. It is a petition supposed to be presented by the dealers in oil, tallow, lamps, &c., in Paris, who request that all shutters, windows, and other apertures for light may be closed against the sun, which spoils their business by shining so brightly during the day. If wheat rained from heaven some people would tax it to protect the farmers. But Free Trade may be made an object of worship in itself, and can then do nothing but harm. It may be made a rule of life, not merely a rule of trade. The satisfaction of material needs is most necessary, and lies at the bottom of civilization, but it is not therefore the most important, and it is quite conceivable that the moral advantages to be derived by a community through reliance on their own energies, may more than compensate for the higher price of particular articles. It has been found not to be good for the human race to have things made too pleasant. The West Indian negroes, "who toil not, neither do they spin," but pick the fruits' of the earth ready to their hands, are not the most exalted specimens of mankind. It may be a good thing for a man *not* to have things too cheaply, if owing to this he is stirred up to work, and can get money enough to live. Free Traders argue that free trade will prevent war, by making evident the inconveniences thereby occasioned to commerce, yet history has never shown that such considerations have been of much weight when strong national feelings are aroused. Nor is it, in my opinion, a desirable thing that they should have a decisive effect. With this class of arguments Free Traders are powerless to deal.

The absence of caste is a noticeable feature in Australian life. Any man, whatever his original position, can rise to the highest offices, and, as a matter of fact, the ministers are frequently tradesmen. None the worse for that, of course; but it was amusingly illustrated in the Assembly the other day, when one of the members—a " chartered libertine," in regard to speech, and they do speak very plainly—boasted that he was a member of a club to which none of the ministers could belong. "They are decent people," he said, " but not professional men, and the membership is limited to them." Domestic servants are particularly independent as a class, and many people do without them altogether rather than submit to pay very high wages for little work. An ordinary cook will receive about £1 a week. They rarely say "sir," but usually plain " mister," which is to most people not a pleasant way of being addressed. They seem to take a pride in addressing their employer (I must not say master or mistress) by their surname, as Mr. or Mrs. So-and-So, as often as possible. What Emerson calls the "fury of expectoration" is very rife throughout the colonies. If a floor or carpet is particularly clean the temptation to spit upon it is too great to be resisted.

In the Court-house at Adelaide is a special notice requesting
people not to spit on the floor. I suppose this habit is connected with smoking, and smoking with drinking. All day
long the hotel bars are besieged by crowds of men demanding
"nobblers," like flies round a pot of honey, and I have heard
that a hotel proprietor does not care to see his customers go
beyond the bar, as so large a proportion of his profit is derived
from it. In a debate in the Assembly, on the new Licensing
Bill, one orator referred contemptuously to "miserable tea
drinkers." "We do not want," he said, "to be Chinafied; the
more men drink the better they are." He would find many
outside the House of the same opinion. *Per contra* it was
urged that total abstinence produced strength because "Samson
was a teetotaller!"

Considering the comparatively small size of Victoria, it is
much more thickly populated than any other colony. Its
population is very nearly a million, on an area about as large
as Great Britain, giving about 10 persons to the square mile.
The chief towns after Melbourne are Ballarat, East and West,
with a population of 37,000, and Sandhurst, with 28,000.
Next comes Geelong, which, with its suburbs, has 21,000.
For purposes of representation, the country is divided into
14 provinces, from each of which three members are returned
to the Legislative Council. It is divided into 55 electoral
districts, which return 86 members to the Legislative Assembly.
The country is also divided into 37 counties, but what purpose

this division serves I have not been able to ascertain. I have made two visits into the country, one to the neighbourhood of Ballarat to the north-west of Melbourne, the other into Gipp's Land, which is to the east. I went to Gipp's Land to pay a visit to a gentleman well known to the racing world, who has a large estate in the neighbourhood of Sale. Victorians are nothing if not fond of sport. We have a good many races at home, but I think they are exceeded in number by those in Victoria. My host had been engaged in horse-racing more than forty years, and in these circles he is much respected; because he always, as they say, runs his horses to win, and the high character he has thus deservedly acquired has done much to raise the morality of the turf in Australia. He told me that he was the second squatter in Gipp's Land. When he first went there in 1841, it took him eighteen days to return to Melbourne through the bush. For six days they had provisions, but for the rest of the time they subsisted on native bears—*i.e.*, sloths. Now he owns about 20,000 acres of the best part of Gipp's Land. Gipp's Land is a large district about twice the size of Wales, which begins at a place called Bunyip, about fifty miles to the east of Melbourne. The train to Sale, the capital—there are two a day—takes about six hours, and the distance is 127 miles. As there are no engineering difficulties, the line did not cost more than £6000 a mile. In many places the gradients are very steep to avoid cuttings. By leaving Melbourne at 6-50 a.m. Sale

F

is reached about 1, and a very tedious and dusty journey
it is. Near Bunyip we pass the borders of an enormous
swamp of 90,000 acres, called Koo-Wee-Rup, which is
about to be drained, and will then form rich agricultural
land. The ride soon becomes monotonous, by reason of the
interminable gum trees. They look very peculiar, being all
dead, and stripped of their leaves and bark, and in the moon-
light show perfectly white. Most of them have been "ringed"
near the bottom to kill them, but others have been killed by
caterpillars. They stand so for a long time. At length they
either fall or are burnt in a bush fire. The flames get inside
the tree, run through it, and come out at the top, as if from a
tall chimney. There are none of great height along the line,
but some trees near Lilydale, about 30 miles north-east of
Melbourne, are supposed to be the highest in the world, and
are above 440 feet in height. In several places are seen
groups of tree ferns some 20 feet high, which form a pleasant
oasis. Gipp's Land did not look its best at the time of my
visit. There had been a drought, more or less, for three years,
and everything was dried up. The cattle appeared parched,
with hard dry skins. Since then, however, there has been a
good deal of rain. Sale itself is an uninteresting town of 3,000
inhabitants, with streets at right angles, and the usual Public
Library and Mechanics' Institute. It also has an artesian well,
which is not usual. Although it was late in the autumn the
heat in the middle of the day was great. In the afternoon it is

tempered by a steady sea breeze. The nights are cool. Along the roads are posts of about four feet high, painted red and white. These are to mark the road in case of a flood, which is not uncommon. From the verandah of my friend's house could be seen a vast extent of rolling upland, dotted pretty thickly with dead gum trees. Fifty years ago it was a dense forest. What may it be fifty years hence, with the increase of population? On the morning after my arrival I was taken a drive over part of the "cattle run." It is only a small run compared to some. The cattle, nearly all bullocks, have about 16,000 acres to wander over. Everywhere the want of water was apparent. I also saw the stables, where were several race-horses, but the best were in the stables at Flemington, near Melbourne. At the end of the week were the Sale races, but I was unable to stay for them, having already made arrangements for a trip to Tasmania.

About six weeks later I went to stay with some friends in the neighbourhood of Ballarat, between that town and Buninyong. I have previously referred to Ballarat as the next largest town to Melbourne. By rail it is 100 miles from Melbourne, though not more than 60 in a direct line. At present the rail goes round by Geelong. Between Geelong and Ballarat the line is double, and admirably constructed, at a cost of £32,000 per mile. It is as well made as any line in England, and the carriages run as smoothly. My friend's house is called "Moramana," a native name, signifying, I am told, "picking up sticks." Buninyong and Ballarat are both native names. It is a matter for discussion whether Ararat, a town some distance to the N.W. of Ballarat, is a native name, too, or whether it has any connection with the ark. I paid a visit to Buninyong, and two visits to Ballarat. Buninyong is properly the name of the mountain there, an extinct volcano, which forms a prominent object in the landscape. The small town takes the same name. It is remarkable chiefly for the fertility of the land in the immediate neighbourhood. It is older than Ballarat, which previous to the discovery of the gold there in 1851 did not exist. There are gold mines, too, at Buninyong, both alluvial and quartz, but chiefly the latter. The Salvation Army flourishes at Buninyong as well as at most places in the Colonies. I have since read in a paper that General Booth has given out that the Salvation Army is likely to become the State church of Victoria, and that Parliament will make it an annual grant of £1,000; or, if not, that Mr. Service will probably do so himself !

Ballarat is a busy town, and here Victorian energy is seen to its best advantage. It is, too, the centre of a large and fertile agricultural district. Gold mining is not now what it once was there. On all sides are the ruins of abandoned "claims," which give a most desolate appearance to the immediate neighbourhood. There is now more gold found at Sandhurst, further north. During the gold fever of 1851, and before there was a line from Geelong, as much as £70 per ton

was paid for carriage from that town. The distance is about
60 miles, and the transit occupied ten days for heavy goods.
" Until last year," said my friend, " there was a man walking
the streets of Ballarat who was known by no other name than
Jimmy. He would never beg and never lie down twice in the
same spot to sleep if others got to know of it. People gave
him food at the door, or, if not, he went to the Asylum for
it. I used to see him taking a zigzag path about the same
time each day. When spoken to he would never reply. He
had been in this condition since thirty years ago. Then he
was a prosperous digger, but some others drugged him, and
took away all his money. The drug spared his life, but took
away his brains; and so he wandered about, always looking
for something, he did not know what." There must be many
similar tales of violence perpetrated during that wild time.
Ballarat contains the widest street in the Colonies—one of the
widest in the world—viz., Sturt-street, which is three chains
wide, but its width is rather concealed by a line of trees in the
middle. There are some fair buildings in it too. Lake
Wendouree, formerly a swamp, now forms a pleasant resort
for the people of Ballarat for boating, and being only four feet
in depth, there is no danger of drowning. The drive round it
too, of about five miles, is pretty. Of course Ballarat cannot
do without an art gallery, but to that much praise cannot be
given. Some of the pictures by local artists may be interesting
as specimens, but the prices attached to them are purely

imaginative. To commemorate the Duke of Edinburgh's visit a public hall was to be built, to which honour both East and West Ballarat—which are separate municipalities—laid claim. The difficulty was solved by building the hall over a small creek which separates the two towns, so that each has one end. As Ballarat is 1,400 feet above Melbourne, the temperature is much lower—10 degrees on an average. When I was there in May the weather was decidedly cold. In winter snow is frequent, while in Melbourne it is the rarest thing. From Ballarat I went to Adelaide, but that must be the subject of another letter.

IV

South Australia.

T is some months since I last wrote about Australia, but it is a question whether something is not gained by a delay in putting together notes of travel. If much is lost in vividness and particularity, yet the whole and its parts are thrown into better proportion, slight incidents that at first seemed of much interest, are relegated to a more humble position, and really salient points have a better chance of receiving their due share of attention.

On the 20th May, I went to Adelaide from Melbourne by the steamer Adelaide, and, among the fine steamers of the Southern Hemisphere, there is none better appointed than this, in respect of food, ventilation, and general comfort. Like many others, it is fitted with the electric light. The captain is a well-known character. Some time before, he had been to blame in a collision with another steamer on the river Yarra,

The Marine Board at Melbourne suspended his certificate for six months, but his employers, I was told, held him in such esteem that during that time he went on his own ship as purser, until he could resume command. I was confined in the cabin with a gentleman, who kindly informed me, beforehand, that he undertook this voyage in order to be sea-sick, on account of his health, and so he kept me in a continual state of expectation, like one who, in the night, every moment expects a cock to crow. At the end of the voyage he expressed his regret that he had not been ill, which I could scarcely share. The journey, by sea, takes about 48 hours; that is, from Port Philip Heads (the entrance to Melbourne Harbour) to Port Adelaide, and the steamers run twice a-week from each end. Soon there will be direct railway communication between Melbourne and Adelaide, but at present the land journey takes three days, and is much more expensive, as a good deal of it has to be done by coaching. The large mail steamers from Europe of the P. & O. and Orient lines stop for a few hours off Glenelg (about seven miles from Adelaide), to land the mails and cargo; but the inter-colonial and other steamers come up, by a long detour, to Port Adelaide, which is also about seven miles from the city; but here they come alongside the wharf. Some of the other colonies have been utilized as penal settlements, or rather begun as such. South Australia was founded consciously and deliberately in 1836. No convict is allowed to land, and a tax of £10 is imposed on every Chinese. The site of Adelaide was chosen for that of the capital. From Port Adelaide to Adelaide the rail runs through a level tract, and the city itself is placed in the centre of a plain, bounded by hills on the north and east at about six miles distance. South Australia appears to be named on the *lucus a non lucendo* principle, because, as a fact, almost the whole of South Australia is to the north of Victoria; and, since 1863, it stretches right across the continent to the north coast of Australia, which is far away into the tropics. Indeed, this northern territory seems to be tacked on to South Australia, because it is not yet of sufficient importance to have a government of its own, and it is difficult to know what to do with it. It is separated by an enormous tract of country, and has nothing in common with South Australia proper. The Bishop told me he supposed he should have to make a visitation through it. If in time this district of the north becomes more populous, it is probable it will set up for itself, just as there have long been agitations for separating Northern Queensland from the Southern portion, and the Riverina from New South Wales, on the ground that their particular interests are not sufficiently represented at Brisbane and Sydney respectively.

The population of the whole of South Australia is now about 318,000, that of Adelaide and its suburbs being about 70,000. Adelaide is not only by far the largest town, but almost the only town of any size. The city is laid out with a regularity that is almost painful. It stands on a square mile

G

of ground. At each side is a terrace, called respectively North, South, East, and West Terrace. There are squares laid out at regular intervals. As is usual in Australian towns, the streets are all at right angles, and generally of the same length and width. The Adelaide people claim to have the finest street in the Colonies, the finest post office, and the best hotel. King William Street is two chains wide—the widest streets in Melbourne are 1½ chains—is a mile long, and contains the principal public buildings, the Town Hall, Post Office, Courts of Justice, &c. The Post Office is a handsome building, with a lofty tower, from which various signs are displayed notifying the arrival and departure of mails. At night the electric light from the top can be seen from a great distance. From King William Street start the various lines of tramway in every direction from the city. They run out to the various suburbs —Magill, Burnside, Kensington, Norwood, Stepney, &c., some of which names sound very familiar. The tramcars are as universally used as in Glasgow, and nowhere have I seen a better service than in Adelaide. It is a pleasant way to spend an afternoon, to ride outside a tramcar in the bright atmosphere, to some suburb, and return after a ramble in the country. From beyond the North Terrace is a capital view over the city. Perhaps the best is from the house of Mr. Way, the Chief Justice. His villa, at which I had the pleasure of visiting him, is one of the most complete I have seen. Nothing is omitted that the arts of civilization can supply. His library contains the choicest modern works. His garden is delicious with cool grottos and fountains. In his aviaries is a collection of the rare birds of the country, all of which he knows. In a separate cage are two fine eagles. Among the flowers I noticed the "Sturt Desert Pea," just then in blossom, the loveliest wild flower of Australia. I have seen houses larger and finer, no doubt, and better collections of particular objects, but never any place so perfect of its kind. Some lines from the "Palace of Art" involuntarily occurred to me, but to no man does the moral of Tennyson's poem less apply than to the Chief Justice, for he is one of the most sympathetic and kind-hearted of men. I had intended staying at the Adelaide Club, and was provided with an introduction, but found on arrival that all the bedrooms were occupied. Besides, visitors are liable to give up their bedrooms to members, and as at this time some races were going on, and the rooms consequently likely to continue occupied, it was better at once to put up at a hotel. This was the "York," which was a comfortable house, and not particularly dear. It is a favourite with visitors by the mail steamers, who often run up from Glenelg for the few hours the steamer calls there.

Like all the other Australian Colonies (except Western Australia) South Australia has a Constitutional Government, established in 1856, consisting of two Houses of Parliament and the Governor. For the Lower House, which has 46 members, there is manhood suffrage. They are not paid as in

Victoria, but a Bill for paying them narrowly escaped passing last session, and will probably be carried soon. While I was there there happened to be an election to the Legislative Council, the Upper House, the members of which retire in rotation. The election address of one candidate is the shortest I have ever seen. It was this: "Gentlemen,—My services are "at your disposal as a candidate for re-election to the Legis- "lative Council." Evidently his constituents were not troubled with burning questions. The position of a Governor in the Colonies is not altogether an enviable one. He has a high official and social position, but little real power, because, practically, he has to consent to any Bill passed by the two Houses. Any one can go to a Governor's reception, and their entertainments are necessarily extremely catholic in their nature. It is matter of common remark that people are seen there who are not seen anywhere else. A Governor's salary is not at all large for his position, and besides general entertaining, he is expected to entertain anyone of the least distinction who may happen to arrive. Adelaide is usually the first calling place for visitors to Australia, and so the Governor of South Australia is peculiarly liable to these calls upon his purse. Every law passed by the Colony has to be ratified at home, so we have a free people at home governing a free people abroad, which is an anomaly, and is daily seen more and more to be so.

South Australia exports wool, wheat, and copper, but the price of copper has fallen more than 50 per cent.; wheat is also very cheap, and has to compete with wheat from India; and in South Australia farming operations are too often conducted by mere " earth scratchers," who have no knowledge of agriculture. In 1851, considerable emigration to Victoria took place in consequence of the discovery of gold in that Colony. There was and is great depression of trade in South Australia, and we have recently heard of the failure of the " Commercial Bank of South Australia," but for all that the amount of the deposits in the South Australian Savings Bank is greater than in any other in proportion to the population. It is nearly £5 per head. It is true some of this is the result of compulsory savings under the provisions of the " Destitute Act."

After a few days at the hotel, I went to stay with a young relative of mine in the northern suburb, where, with one exception, I remained the rest of my time. His wife kept no servant, not so much on account of the expense as because, as she said, " They are more bother than they're worth," and indeed this is a universal complaint in the Colonies. I slept in a small room, and the last night but one observed in a corner of the ceiling, above the bed, what seemed to be a large spider. On mentioning this the next morning, I learnt that it was a tarantula, and was of use in catching insects. " Oh, but," I said, " doesn't it come down at night?" " Oh, no," said my friend, " it never comes below *this*," marking a spot about a yard above my head. This was not very reassuring, as there appeared nothing to prevent the animal from transgressing the prescribed limit, should it feel so disposed. It never troubled me however, but I was afterwards told that it had once come down too far and been killed. Such animals are unpleasant, and at times dangerous, but they may be expected in countries where the heat is as great as it is in Adelaide, which is considered to be one of the hottest places in the globe inhabited by man. One evening we went to hear the Bishop preach in the Cathedral. It is a very unpretending edifice, and in fact is only half built. It is all choir and no nave. In consequence of the great number of women who attend the services, or of the politeness of the men, or both, the Bishop has been obliged to set apart seats for men to protect them against the encroachment of what Mr. Swinburne calls the "stronger sex." Another evening we went to see a native dance or "corrobboree" as it is called. There are not many natives now left in South Australia, and what there are have become very degraded. The law forbids the sale to them of intoxicating liquors. Spirits not merely make them drunk, but drive them mad. As a sort of compensation they come down to Adelaide at stated times for blankets, which are distributed to them by the Government. On these occasions they are accustomed to exhibit themselves in their native antics and dances for a little gain. At this time was expected a large muster, and in order to accommodate as many visitors as possible, the Adelaide Cricket Club had induced the natives to hold their corrobboree on the cricket ground, of course themselves looking for a large money return. Certainly their anticipations must have been more than fulfilled, for there was a crowd at the entrance resembling that outside a London theatre on boxing night. Instead of 3,000 people, the number expected, there were nearer 15,000. Seats in the grand stand were 1s., outside the ring was 6d., but soon all distinction of place was lost. Presently about 50 natives, hideously decorated, and stained with red to represent gashes on the head and breast, filed into the enclosure in a long line. Small bonfires were lighted at intervals, and on these the performers leapt, one exactly following the steps of another. Then they imitated the bounds of the Kangaroo when pursued, but of dancing, or even posturing, in our sense of the word, there was none. Meantime the "lubras" (native women) seated on the ground in one mass, kept up a monotonous chant, varying their cadences with the beat of tom-toms. The night was dark, and the figures were indistinctly seen. Soon the vast crowd becoming impatient, burst through the barriers, and scattered the burning brands. A great scene of confusion ensued, and the performance came abruptly to an end. One of the blacks remarked, not without reason, "Me tink dis white fellows' corrobboree." It is a painful thing to see a race so degenerate as to be willing to show themselves for money before their supplanters, and to see the former "lords of the soil" begging a copper from the passer-by. One cannot but desire that their extinction in these parts, which is certain, may be also speedy.

I cannot easily imagine two more pitiable objects than those I afterwards saw at Albany in Western Australia : a native man and woman begging, standing with their shrunken limbs in rags that barely covered them. The cricket ground is in the "reserve," a part between the north terrace and the northern suburb, which belongs to the community and cannot be built on. It is separated from the north terrace by the river Torrens. Like many Australian rivers, the Torrens starts up in various places and does not seem to have either a beginning or an ending. It might be compared to the "sullen mole that runneth underneath," between Letherhead and Dorking ; but these Australian rivers, when they do appear, are inclined to stagnate. The municipality of Adelaide, however, have wisely dammed up the river, and converted it into a lake of about one and a half miles long, thus improving an eyesore into an ornament. It is spanned by a handsome bridge. Near the north terrace, too, are the Botanical Gardens, one of the best in Australia. The Zoological Gardens are close by, where there is a black cockatoo and a white peacock.

As I said before, Adelaide is the only town of any size. There are others, however. One day I went with my friend by train to the small town of Gawler, which is about 25 miles to the north. The train takes about one and a half hours. There we were met by a gentleman with a trap, who took us to see an ostrich farm about four miles from Gawler. It belongs to a company at Adelaide and we had an order from head quarters to be shown over it. Ostriches have been imported into South

Australia from the Cape of Good Hope, and thrive here well enough. At length, seeing the risk of a sharp competition in ostrich feathers, the Cape authorities have laid an embargo of £100 on every ostrich exported, but this is locking the stable door when the horse has escaped, for there are now in South Australia quite sufficient birds to keep up the breed. The farm manager was a dry old Scotchman of much humour, and had made himself accustomed to their ways. The farm was about 170 acres in extent, and at this time there were about 100 ostriches upon it, a number having recently been sent away north to Port Augusta, where is another farm belonging to the same Company. Some of the birds had committed suicide on their way to the sea. They will run up against palings or wire, get their long necks entangled, and sometimes cut their throats in trying to extricate themselves. I noticed one that had his throat bandaged up on this account. The birds are kept in paddocks, three or four together, or more, if young and tame, but some are very savage. We drove through all the paddocks, but the manager kept a sharp look-out, lest any should "bounce" at us. An ostrich, in attacking, kicks forward with his legs, which give tremendous blows, and then, when he has kicked down his enemy, he will probably sit upon him, and his weight is about two hundredweight. An ostrich, therefore, cannot be considered a generous foe. The old manager had been a good deal knocked about by them himself. On one occasion a bird had kicked him twice, broken a rib or two, and got him

H

up fast against the palings. However, he managed to seize hold of the bird's neck, and calling to some men on the other side, he handed the neck to them over the palings, to hold while he made his escape—which his ingenuity certainly deserved. I asked him what he did when they ran away, " Well," he said, " I sit down and wait till they stop; you can't catch them." The male takes turn with the female in sitting on the eggs, and when an ostrich has young ones she is very dangerous to approach. A good breeding couple are worth £300. The feathers are not taken off at any particular time of the year, but as they are ready, nor is cruelty exercised in taking them. I saw several ovens which had been used for hatching the eggs, but now they have enough birds to let them be hatched naturally, which is the safer way. An ostrich at close quarters is certainly an unpleasant looking beast ; his neck, moving rapidly in all directions, surmounted by a small head, with bright wicked-looking eyes, reminds one of a snake. He has a fancy for anything bright, and will make for a button on your coat if it happens to gleam. I asked the age of ostriches, but could obtain no information. They look wiry enough to live for ever.

On our return to Gawler we called on the way to see an orange farm. The oranges were being picked. The trees, laden with fruit, seemed to have repaid the labour of the cultivator. Oranges require a great deal of water. This grove was in a sheltered valley, and water was supplied by a pump worked by wind. The man with us said you could not tell exactly

what sort of oranges would come, because the same tree sometimes bears different kinds. Whether this is the case I do not
know. Paramatta, near Sydney, is the chief place for oranges
in Australia, but these of Gawler seemed to be as good as any
we could desire, to judge from the taste. At Gawler we had
tea at a friend's house. He said amongst other things—all
interesting, but which I have forgotten—that he always gave
tramps a meal (which seems to be the custom) and usually
offered them work, but that none would work for less than 4s. 6d.
a day. They preferred to do nothing. The Gawler Museum
was close by. It contains native clubs, tom-toms, skins of
fishes, and a valuable book of engravings from Hogarth. The
last two or three days of my visit to South Australia I spent
with an old friend, who has been about six years a Professor at the University. He lived about 20 miles to the east
of Adelaide, beyond the Mount Lofty range, and the scenery by
rail thither, across the mountains, is very striking. His comfortable house is about a mile from the station, and here he
spends his leisure time with his family, in sensible pursuits.
The University of Adelaide is yet in its early youth, and only
quite lately have any buildings been erected for it, but the
professorships are well endowed, and the number of students
annually increases. From Adelaide I returned by steamer to
Melbourne, and from there in a few days I went to Tasmania.
On my subsequent return to England I spent a day at Adelaide,
but then was in the company of friends the whole time.

V.

Tasmania.

HE island of Tasmania is about 200 miles direct South of Victoria. Up to 1856 its name was Van Diemen's land. Then it was officially changed to Tasmania, a name which is more euphonious and at the same time more correct, for the island was discovered by the Dutch navigator, Tasman, who called it after his father-in-law, Van Diemen. The change of name does not seem at once to have been appreciated in England, for it is related of the first Bishop of Tasmania, Bishop Nixon that, having occasion to call at the Foreign Office, he left his card "F. R. Tasmania," and received a reply addressed to F. R. Tasmania, Esq.! This reminds one of the Duke of Newcastle, who, when Prime Minister, expressed his astonishment that Cape Breton was an island, and hurried off to tell the King. Tasmania may be reached direct from England by the Steamers of the Shaw Savill and Albion

Line, which call at Hobart on their way to New Zealand once
a month. The Steamers of the New Zealand Shipping Co.
also call occasionally at Hobart for coal, but they are not to
be relied on for stopping. Tasmania is however usually reached
from Melbourne. Bass's Straits, the sea between Victoria and
Tasmania is usually stormy, and many passengers who have
never been seasick all the way from England have succumbed
to Bass's Straits. What is more remarkable however, is that
some for whom Bass's Straits have had no terrors, have been sea-
sick on the narrow-gauge line from Launceston to Hobart!
There are two ways of going from Melbourne to Hobart, one
by Steamer to Launceston at the north of the Island, and 40
miles up the river Tamar, which takes about 24 hours, and
thence by express train to Hobart which takes $5\frac{3}{4}$ hours, the
other by Steamer all the way. There are two lines of Steamers,
the Tasmanian S.S. Co., and the Union S.S. Co., of New
Zealand, which calls at Hobart on the way to New Zealand.
The Steamers of the latter Company are built by Messrs.
Denny, of Dumbarton, and are fine, comfortable, and swift.
To travel by one of them is in my opinion far the pleasantest
way of reaching Hobart from Melbourne. Others to whom the
shortest sea passage is preferable, will naturally go by Launceston, and will have a beautiful ride through the country, though
they may be shaken to pieces.

Tasmania is about half the size of England, but its population is only 120,000. There are only two towns of any size

—Hobart in the south and Launceston in the north. A great
deal of the interior is marshy, and there are lakes of some considerable size, which in the winter are sometimes frozen. The
north-west coast is very barren and sparsely inhabited. The
doctors and clergy in these parts have often long journeys to
make through the bush. In climate, Tasmania is preferable to
Australia. The temperature is much more equable, and therefore not so trying to weak constitutions. Formerly, many
Anglo-Indians visited the north-west coast; but this has not
been so much the case latterly. Numbers of tourists come
from Australia during the summer months. Compared to the
larger island, Tasmania is well watered, and the rainfall is
very much greater. The climate has often been compared
to that of England, without its damps and fogs, but the
lightness and clearness of the atmosphere rather resemble that
of the South of France or Italy, and supply that gentle exhilara-
tion to the spirits which can be so seldom known in England.
Mount Wellington, which rises 4,000 feet above Hobart, is
often covered with a wreath of mist, and in the winter with
snow. Many English fruits and trees have been introduced,
and flourish well. The sweet briar was brought in some years
ago, and now in many parts the hedges are of nothing else.
The native foliage is, however, the same as that of Australia.
Everywhere the eucalyptus predominates, and in Tasmania
grows to a great height. Some of the finest trees may be seen
in driving from Hobart along the Huon Road.

Up to within the last five and thirty years, the history of Tasmania was that of a penal settlement. Much has been written of the convict life, which it is not necessary to repeat here. I have often heard that Marcus Clarke's powerful but repulsive tale, " His Natural Life" is strictly true, even in its most horrible details. To the evils inherent in the system, others seem to have been deliberately added by the authorities. The convicts were employed as servants, and it was even permitted to a free woman to marry a convict, and then if he displeased her, she might have him punished. The buildings of the settlement at Port Arthur are still standing, but are fast falling into ruin. On the ceiling of the chapel there are yet to be seen marks of blood from the floggings there inflicted. The old doors and bolts of cells are used by the people in their own houses. It was of frequent occurrence that convicts effected an escape, but they were usually compelled, through hunger, to give themselves up. In cases where several escaped, they became bushrangers, and rendered travelling in the interior unsafe, for, their lives being already forfeited, they had no motive to abstain from pillage and murder. It appears that one at least of the Governors of the convict establishments, took a malicious pleasure in taunting those under his care. At length he fell a victim to his own conduct. It may be a question whether it would not have been better to hang a man at once than to transport him to Van Dieman's Land; but there can be no question whatever that to class one who had been guilty of some petty theft, with the abandoned wretches that convicts speedily become, is a deed of which the wickedness can hardly be exaggerated. The system, too, had a bad effect upon the free inhabitants. While the convicts were no better than slaves, in the masters were engendered some of the autocratic habits of slave-owners. If a convict gave the slightest offence to his master or mistress, nothing was easier than to send him with a note to the nearest magistrate, requesting that the bearer might receive fifty lashes. The spirit of caste would soon be manifested. The free white population would despise the convicts, or children of convicts—perhaps also the poor free whites. These distinctions have long ceased, but the feelings associated with them are not so easily eradicated. Even now the descendants of convicts are sometimes secretly looked down upon, and a great many have, on that account, left the island. Much public work has been done by convict labour. If a road is particularly well made, it is a sure remark that it was made by the "Government stroke," but as a monument of human industry, slave labour does not impress the mind like free labour. One does not contemplate the pyramids of Egypt with the same satisfaction as St. Peter's or St. Paul's. An account of the present aborigines of Tasmania may be given with the same brevity as that of the snakes in Ireland—there are none. The last was an old woman who died about ten years ago. They were gradually reduced in numbers, partly by the invaders, partly by natural causes, and at last the remnant was deported to one of the neighbouring islands. In 1854 there were only 16 left. In the museum at Hobart are portraits of a good many, with unpronounceable names. By the Australians, Tasmania is sometimes called "sleepy hollow," and certainly, compared with their neighbours across the water, the Tasmanians do appear to be deficient in energy. The revenue of the country is, indeed, increasing, though slowly. There are now only about 400,000 acres under cultivation. A great many sheep are imported from Victoria. The principal manufacture is jam, but the customs duties of Victoria put difficulties in the way of a large export. Lately, the tin mines of Mount Bischoff, in the N.W., have been exceedingly productive, but there is an immense amount of mineral wealth in Tasmania not yet tapped. With the exception of Newfoundland, it is, I believe, the only Colony not represented at the present Colonial and Indian Exhibition, and this must be matter of regret to all wellwishers of the island, because it it certainly not due to want of materials for exhibition. There might be shown the varieties of the gum tree, the beautiful tree-ferns, the pretty shells which are made into necklaces, the skin of the black opossum, of which the finest opossum rugs are made (the black opossum has, however, become very rare, and brown skins are sometimes dyed black). There is, too, the Tasmanian devil, a small but formidable animal, something like a badger, and the ornithorhynchus, or duck-billed platypus, which figures on some of the postage stamps. This want of energy is

I

a fact, however it may be accounted for. Probably the emigration to Australia of some of the convict families, as above
mentioned, has withdrawn some useful members of society.
Again, in 1851, the discovery of gold in Victoria attracted the
most adventurous spirits from the other Colonies, and from Tasmania among the rest. It is true that much of the dangerous and
criminal element in the population may thus have been removed,
but, at the same time, the young blood went with it, and, as
Pericles said, to take the young away from a city is like taking
the spring out of the year, and now many of the young men go to
Australia or elsewhere to seek their fortunes, a fact which may
be considered as much an effect of the present stagnation as a
cause of it. Throughout the island generally the usual proportion of the sexes is maintained, but in Hobart the female
sex appears to have a decided preponderance. Tasmania, and
especially Hobart, has had a reputation for the beauty of the
women; Anthony Trollope and other writers mention it. Many
men from Melbourne have brought their wives from across the
the straits. I am bound to say that my own observation
scarcely bore out this tradition, but one must be very insensible
not to admire the fresh and clear complexions both of women
and men ; they have the same complexions as we see in
England, than which there cannot be higher commendation.
Although the total population of Tasmania is so small, the
machinery of government is large. There is a Governor, a
Legislative Council of 16 members, and a Legislative Assembly

of 32 members. Both houses are elective, though not with the same suffrage; but as even the lower house is not elected by manhood suffrage, the constitution is not so democratic as that of Victoria. During my visit the chief political question was the defence of the island against possible Russian attack. The artillery were daily practising at Kangaroo Point, which commands the entrance to Hobart. The present acting Chief Justice had been Premier and Attorney General for five years previously, and had brought the finances into a satisfactory state. Each minister has a salary of £700. The High Court of Justice consists of a Chief Justice and a Puisne Judge. The result of this is that there is virtually no appeal from the decision of a single judge; because, if even on appeal the Court should be divided, the previous judgment must necessarily be confirmed. The only appeal, therefore, is to the Judicial Committee of the Privy Council, a proceeding which would probably be attended with too much expense to be ever resorted to. The two branches of the legal profession—Barristers and Solicitors—are amalgamated, but in practice they are usually kept distinct. A jury consists of seven, of whom a majority of five can give a verdict.

Education is well endowed in Tasmania. There is as yet no University, though attempts have been made to found one, but the Council of Education confers the degree of Associate of Arts, and every year two scholarships, called the "Tasmanian Scholarships," of the value of £200 per annum, each

for four years, to be held at any British university, are awarded
if the candidates pass satisfactorily the required examination.
This is indeed a splendid scholarship. There are various other
scholarships for boys and girls under the age of 12, and others
for those under 15, so that it is possible for a boy to rise " from
the gutter to the University." The recent success of girls has
brought forward the question whether they too should not be
allowed to compete for the Tasmanian Scholarship. Newspapers may be sent post free to Great Britain or the other
colonies, to promote, I presume, knowledge of the country. The
telephone is much more in use than in England, and is frequently used in place of the telegraph. The cost of it is only
£6 per annum. Nor in railway communication is Tasmania
behind. I mean that there are enough railways to keep up
with the requirements of the country, but new lines are being
made, and they of course will create fresh requirements. The
principal line is that connecting Launceston with Hobart. It
belongs to a private company, but the Government guaranteed
5 per cent. on the cost of construction up to £650,000. That
sum was not sufficient, and subsequently £100,000 and
£50,000 had to be borrowed to complete the line. The
present income is about £70,000—a large amount for the
small population at each end and on the way. Therefore when
the chairman at the recent meeting of shareholders in London
anticipated an income of £150,000, he was rather in the
clouds. The line is 133 miles in length, and has a gauge of

3ft. 6in.   It passes through some beautiful scenery, especially towards the Hobart end, and the numerous bends of the line give travellers an excellent opportunity for seeing the country. To one not used to it, however, the jolting is most unpleasant, and the pace kept up round the curves is too great for safety. Indeed, there have lately been some fatal accidents on that very account.   Among the stations are Jerusalem and Jericho, before which the line skirts the Lake of Tiberias.   Not far off is Bagdad—which also has its Caliph.   There is one express train a day each way, which keeps up an average speed of 23 miles per hour.   Launceston has about 15,000 inhabitants, and is a more business-like town than Hobart.   Otherwise it is not particularly interesting.   Hobart, which up to 1881 was called Hobart Town, has a most enchanting situation.   The scenery is of that ideal nature which, especially when the afternoon sun gleams on the water and the hills, reminds the spectator (if it is not contradictory to say so) of the "Light that never was on sea or land."

Hobart lies about seven miles from the sea, which here runs up into the land like a Norwegian fiord, and at the mouth of the river Derwent.   It is built upon sloping ground, between the river and Mount Wellington, a huge mass that dwarfs every other object.   Each side of this fiord are green hills, from any one of which are charming views of sea and land.   The town much resembles an English country town.   The streets are narrower than those of Australian towns, and though mostly at right angles are not so painfully regular. They are mostly named after past Governors, as Macquarie Street, Davey Street, Collins Street, Franklin Square, etc. Over the Town Hall a flag flies, with the proud motto "*Sic fortis Hobartia crevit,*" and the arms of the city, supported by a kangaroo and an emu. Under this same roof is the Public Library, containing about 10,000 volumes. The chief English periodicals are taken here. I remember reading here Froude's "Carlyle in London," which is a biography worthy to stand beside Boswell. It is a real biography, not a mere jumble of undigested letters and diary thrown before the public, which is too much the modern notion of writing Somebody's Life. Hobart has none of the cosmopolitanism of Melbourne. Its habits are essentially provincial—what the Germans call *Kleinstädtisch*. There is a small theatre at Hobart, to which companies sometimes come from Melbourne. I saw the "Ticket-of-Leave Man" here. The audience, which almost entirely consisted of the pit, were still in that primitive stage of criticism in which the villain (who was a good actor) was hooted, and the honest man (an indifferent actor) vehemently applauded. I remember asking the way to the theatre of a bearded individual, who turned out to be an officer of the Salvation Army. "Ah, sir!" he said, "We don't believe in theatres, we're booked for Heaven"—a most comfortable conviction to carry through this life, whatever may be the ultimate issue. Lying as it does in the midst of such beautiful scenery, Hobart is a good centre from which to make excursions. A favourite place for picnics is Brown's River, about 10 miles away, the road following the water edge along "Sandy Bay." An Antipodean picnic is nothing without tea. In fact the tea-pot is the centre round which everything revolves. The first thing to be done is to collect wood for a fire. The "billy" is then filled with water and set to boil. Meantime those not connected with these preliminaries wander through the woods or along the shore. At a picnic to Brown's River I saw the famous cherries with the stones growing outside. It certainly is a kind of fruit with the stone outside, but bears no resemblance whatever to the cherry. Near Brown's River is the Blow Hole. This is an opening at the bottom of a rock, through which at certain states of the tide the water rushes, I presume, with much noise and violence, but when I saw it all was quiet. For a two days excursion from Hobart, none can be better than to take the coach along the Huon Road to Victoria, at the head of the Huon River, sleep there, and the next morning take the steamer from Victoria down the small river, along the D'Entrecasteaux channel between the island of Bruni and the mainland, and so back to Hobart. I had arranged for this trip with a friend, and had gone so far as to consult the "Captain of the Pinafore," (the tiny craft above alluded to), as to the time of starting from Victoria, for she does not start every day, but an accident at the last moment prevented us. Subsequently, however, I had in a drive a good opportunity of seeing the best of the scenery along the Huon Road. Along the Huon River I am told there are hermits. At any rate there is one man who has not been seen for nine years. He brings any fruit he has to sell to a certain spot and lights a fire. This is seen, and in exchange for his commodities food is left for him.

Another beautiful trip from Hobart is a journey of 20 miles up the river Derwent to New Norfolk. The steamer takes about three hours. About halfway the river is crossed by the main line railway at Bridgewater, and up to this point is of a considerable width. On the North the river skirts the wooded sides of Mount Direction, on the South Mount Wellington almost fills up the landscape. After passing Bridgewater the river much narrows, and further on the woods descend to the water's edge in some places, reminding the traveller of the Dart between Dartmouth and Totnes. Just before reaching New Norfolk a huge rock, called from its shape the Pulpit Rock, quite overhangs the river. A branch line from Bridgewater to New Norfolk was being made along the North side, close to the water's edge, and now the Pulpit Rock has been removed, for though a picturesque object it looked dangerous, and everything must, of course, give way to railways. On landing at the wharf at New Norfolk, a boy came forward and offered to drive me to the well-known salmon ponds, where, for a good many years, attempts have been made to rear salmon from ova brought from England, but it is doubtful whether they

have met with success. Small fish have certainly been raised,
but the question is whether they are salmon, and it is said none
have attained a size sufficiently large to solve the enigma. The
distance is only a few miles, and the drive is pretty, but ten
shillings was too much for the pleasure of a solitary journey, for
there was no one else likely to be a passenger in the winter time.
New Norfolk lies pleasantly situated in a valley on the South
side of the Derwent. The soil is favourable for hops, which
have been introduced from England, and grow well here. I
have been told that the freight of hops from Tasmania to
England is less than the carriage from some parts of Kent to
London ; but as the carriage, say from Maidstone to London,
is about one and sixpence per pocket, they could be carried at
such a rate from Tasmania only as a back freight, and when
the owner wants anything to fill up. For the night I put up at
the " Bush," the favourite and principal inn, but now I was the
only guest. After dark I started out to see the little township,
but as the moon was only in its first quarter, and there was no
artificial light, not much could be made out then. Launceston
and Hobart are the only towns that have gas, and while the
moon is shining, or is due to shine, even that is not lighted—
a piece of economy that may be excused where gas is about ten
shillings per thousand. The next day I returned by land to
Hobart, travelling to Bridgewater by a top-heavy coach, which
at every turn sent my heart into my mouth, but it was skilfully
driven.

K

Tasmania cannot be said to have progressed much of late years, yet it does make progress, and is not now receding as it was when Sir C. Dilke visited it about 20 years ago. I do not know that any land is now allowed to go out of cultivation as was then the case. It has not been entirely its own fault either. The protective duties of Victoria have much checked the exportation of fruit and jam. The question of Protection *versus* Free Trade is a permanent subject of controversy in the Colonies. At the present moment the Premier of Victoria is a Free Trader, while the Chief Secretary is an ardent Protectionist. If this difference of opinion exists in the most advanced and populous colony, what certainty of policy can be looked for in the others? The best solution would probably be an intercolonial Zollverein, towards which events seem to be tending. Whether eventually it will include Great Britain is a part of the wider question of Federation. That Tasmania is a country with many resources—especially mineral wealth—as yet undeveloped, is a conclusion at which most people will arrive, even after a short visit to the colony; but, how soon and in what way this development will take place depends, of course, upon the character of the inhabitants, and this character will, no doubt, improve as the remembrances of the convict life, which has so blighted this beautiful island, gradually recede into the dim distance of the past.

VI

Auckland and Sydney.

DO not know that I have any right to say anything about New Zealand, seeing that I was only three days upon the North Island. I had indeed intended to have paid a proper visit. I had intended seeing the famous pink and white terraces (now alas! destroyed), and the rest of the lake district; and at various places I had a good many introductions from friends. But the force of circumstances—sometimes said to be another name for weakness of will—intervened, and my fine schemes ended ingloriously in a flying visit to Auckland, on a business matter.

I have before alluded to the excellent steamers of the Union S.S. Co., of New Zealand. This Company appears to have a monopoly of the trade between Australia and New Zealand, and if their steamers continue as they now are there is not much reason to fear competition. They start from Melbourne, call at Hobart, run across to the South of the island of New Zealand, then, calling at the principal ports along the whole length of the east coast of the two islands till they reach Auckland, they steam straight across to Sydney. The same journey is made back again from Sydney to Melbourne. The route is sometimes varied, but this is the usual course. The names of their steamers are from lakes in New Zealand, Tarawera, Wairarapa, Te Anau, &c., while the steamers of the New Zealand Shipping Co. are named from mountains, as Tongariro, Aorangi, Rimutaka, &c. On the day that I had arranged to leave Hobart by the Union line for New Zealand, it happened that one of the New Zealand Co.'s steamers called in for coal, and as this steamer—a fine vessel of 4,000 tons—was going direct to Auckland it suited me much better. She had come round the Cape, thus avoiding the heat of the Suez Canal. This is a monthly service direct to New Zealand. The Shaw Savill and Albion Line also has a monthly service, so that every fortnight there is a steamer direct from England arriving in New Zealand. The sea was smooth, and consequently the passage was quick. On the morning of the third day we passed the Snares Rocks, to the south of Stewart's Island. On the fifth, the snowy sides of the Kaikoura mountains were glittering in the morning sun as we passed a few miles from shore, and about 4 o'clock on the morning of the eighth day, we were alongside the wharf in the spacious harbour of Auckland. Close by, my eye was caught by the "Ohau," a small steamer, which, as it happened, I had seen launched about nine months previously at Dumbarton—little expecting to see it again.

It is doubtful whether New Zealand belongs geographically to Australia or to the Pacific Islands. It is said that some shocks of earthquake in New Zealand have been felt in Tas-. mania. On the other hand there is above a thousand miles of rough sea between Australia and New Zealand, with no connecting islands between, and nature presents quite a different aspect in the two countries. The gum tree is the principal tree on the Australian continent, the Kauri pine in New Zealand. In the latter country there are no kangaroos, no emus, no snakes, in fact very few indigenous animals. The bones of a gigantic bird, the moa, are to be found, but the bird itself has long been extinct. Every variety of climate and scenery may be found in New Zealand. The winter of the South Island is as rigorous as that of England, while the North Island nearly reaches the tropics. In the North Island are the famous hot lakes ; in the South the very lofty range of mountains known as the Southern Alps, which attains a height of 13,000 feet in Mount Cook. The scenery on the South-west coast, from Milford Sound downwards, where the sea runs up many miles into the land, and the steamer passes through narrow straits between perpendicular walls of rock, has often been compared to that of the wilder fiords of Norway. It is little more than forty years since New Zealand was colonized by Europeans, but already shoals of books have been written about it. The Maoris, as is well known, are not the original inhabitants. Their traditions relate—and they are confirmed by independent investigations—that they came about 400 years ago from the South Sea Islands, and drove out or exterminated the natives. As a fact the Maoris are immeasurably superior to the Australian natives. Captain Cook, in describing his landing in 1769, says, "one of the natives raised his spear, as if to dart it at the boat; the coxswain fired, and shot him dead,"—a melancholy omen of the future relations between the natives and the strangers. The Maori wars have cost us many lives, but, of course, have always had the same ending. The natives have gradually been straitened in room, and their numbers have steadily declined. It is true that the census of 1881 shows a rather larger number of natives (44,000 odd) than in 1858, but in the latter year it was probably not so accurately made, and there is little doubt that they are now rapidly diminishing. They are nearly all in the North Island, in the neighbourhood of the Hot Lake district. The portion specially alloted to them is called the King Country, and no European may enter this without permission. Thus they have prevented the ascent of Mount Tongariro, which is *tapu*, or sacred. They are now much better treated than formerly, and send four members to Parliament. In their language there is no *s* or *f*, vowels are very numerous, and every word ends with a vowel. The sound of the words, therefore, is easy and flowing, and the native names are far more euphonious than those of Australia.

There is already a good deal of literature about the Maoris, their habits and customs and religious ideas. No doubt they are of the widely-spread Malay race, which has over-run the South Pacific. The religious notions of the most different races in a certain stage of civilization much resemble one another. We know, for instance, that the Greeks of Homer's time (whatever that was) besides worshipping the gods of Olympus, identified every ruin, mountain, or cape with some superhuman person—whether demon, or hero, or nymph. So we read (in Wakefield's adventures in New Zealand) that the chief Heu-Heu appeals to his ancestor the great mountain Tongariro, "I am the Heu-Heu, and rule over you all just as my ancestor, Tongariro, the mountain of Snow, stands above all this land." Heu-Heu refused permission to anyone to ascend the mountain, on the ground that it was his *tipuna* or ancestor,—"he constantly identified himself with the mountain, and called it his sacred ancestor." The mountains in New Zealand are accounted by the natives male and female. Tarawera and Taranaki, two male mountains, once quarrelled about the affections of a small volcanic female mountain in the neighbourhood. A great deal about the transactions between the New Zealand Government and the natives may be learnt from the recent interesting libel action of *Bryce* v. *Rusden*, in which the former, who has been native minister in the Government, recovered

£5000 damages against the defendant, the author of a History of New Zealand. Up to 1876 the islands were divided into nine provinces, each of which had a separate Council, subject to the central Government at Wellington, but in that year the provincial Councils were abolished, and the Government is now like that of the Australian Colonies, with a governor and two houses of Parliament. The members of the Lower House are paid. In "Greater Britain," Sir Charles Dilke, making a contrast between New Zealand and Australia, suggests that New Zealand is aristrocratic and Australia democratic. To me they appeared equally democratic. The payment of members is an advanced step even in a democracy.

Auckland is by far the largest town in the North Island, with its suburbs, now containing nearly 50,000 inhabitants. Up to 1864 it was also the seat of Government, but that was then moved to Wellington as being a more central town. There is much rivalry between Auckland and Dunedin, the largest town in the South Island. Dunedin is the capital of the pro-provincial district of Otago, which is chiefly inhabited by Scotch, or people of Scotch descent. The Scotch have the great merit of sticking to their friends. If there is anything to be done or gained, a Scotchman naturally gets the preference. I heard an amusing illustration of this on the way to New Zealand. At one of the ports in Otago a steamer required new boilers, and tenders were asked for. One was much lower than the others, and was accepted. The name of the contractor appeared to be

Macpherson, but when sent for he turned out to be a China-man. He had been shrewd enough to see that he had no chance of getting the work in his own name. The total population of New Zealand is a little over 500,000, and the public debt is about £37,000,000. This seems to show that taxation must be high. A good deal of this large amount has, it is true, been expended on railways, which all belong to the State, and therefore the burden, though heavy, is not quite so heavy as it appears at first sight. A friend at Auckland told me that New Zealand is a paradise for working-men and for men with capital, who can safely lend it at a high rate of interest. It is probably, too, a capital place for domestic servants, who everywhere in the Colonies seems to have pretty much their own way. I have also heard that dentists are much in request. A lady, living near Auckland, had to drive twelve miles, and then put her name down in a book three weeks beforehand, to see the dentist! But for people who want to find something to do, and have no money and no manual skill, the prospect is not so smiling. For instance, I should not imagine that teaching is a lucrative pursuit—private teaching that is to say, for in public teaching the supply is in excess of the demand, and, no doubt, rightly so, in a young community. New Zealand annually spends on education £500,000, or £1 per head of the population, a higher proportion than is spent by any other country. Formerly there was the University of Otago and the University of New Zealand, but the former has now ceased to

L

have the power of conferring degrees, and has been virtually
amalgamated with the University of New Zealand. This
University has affiliated colleges at Auckland, Wellington,
Christchurch, and Dunedin, though the latter is still styled
the University of Otago. Each of these colleges has a
staff of highly-paid professors, with not much to do as
yet in the strict line of business, to judge by the number
of students. But of course the taste for advanced education
has to be created before it can be much in request. The
salaries are large enough to tempt over some of the best
men from England, but a professor is expected to come out as
a public man much more here than at home. He is expected to
deliver a course of lectures in public, to entertain socially, and
to interest himself in local affairs. At Auckland they boasted
that on their School Board they had a Senior Classic and a
Senior Wrangler.

Auckland is, as I said, the only town I actually visited
in New Zealand. Of the town itself there is not much to be
said. It is not particularly interesting, and the climate is
rather relaxing ; when it rains the roads are almost impassable
with mud. But its situation is most charming from its beauty,
and most advantageous for trade. The harbour of Auckland
is thought by some to rival that of Sydney for beauty and
commodiousness. From the summit of Mount Eden, an extinct
volcano, with a perfectly formed crater (its extinction, however,
does not appear so certain, after the recent experience of

Mount Tarawera, which was thought to be equally extinct), an extensive view of Auckland and the two seas is to be obtained. For at this point the North Island is so narrow, that Manukau harbour on the west side comes close up to Auckland, and at one point the distance across is only a mile and a half. There has been a project mooted to cut through the narrow isthmus, and thus lessen the journey to Sydney by about 300 miles, but all the harbours of New Zealand lie towards the Pacific, not towards Australia, and there is a formidable bar at the entrance to Manukau harbour, so that after all the expense would probably be too great. Auckland is on the direct track for steamers from San Francisco to Sydney, and up to last year there was a regular service of three steamers, once a month—I forget the name of the line. Many went by this route, as the fare from Sydney to London this way is only £66, including the rail across America, but there were many complaints of the inferiority of the steamers. That line has now ceased, but the Union Line of New Zealand now run their steamers along the same route, and, I believe, have a subsidy from New Zealand and New South Wales for the mail service to America. It was by one of the steamers of the former line, the "Zealandia," that I left Auckland for Sydney on the 28th June. The voyage took five days over a calm sea, and was quite without incident. We were, however, enlivened by the presence of Mr. Dion Boucicault, the well-known playwright and actor, with his company, who were on their way to fulfil engagements in Melbourne and Sydney, after some years stay in America; we had many amusing, but highly-coloured anecdotes. Among them one alone, told by an actor who died sadly and suddenly at Melbourne a few weeks later, now remains in my memory. Some time previously he had been acting at Ottawa, and the play was Richard III. He was Richmond, and in reply to his speech the Duke of Norfolk says, "Your words are fire, my lord, and warm our men." On this occasion the army consisted of one man, one woman (dressed as a soldier) and a boy, and the very conscientious duke replied, "Your words are fire, my lord, and warm our *man*." I tell it as it was told me, but my friend must have made some mistake. These words do not occur in Shakespeare's Richard III. (though they may in the acting version) and at any rate there is no conversation between Richmond and the Duke of Norfolk.

On arrival at Sydney I made no stay, but returned to Melbourne the next day by steamer. However, I paid my visit of five weeks to Sydney a short time afterwards. This time I left Melbourne by the very fine steamer Buninyong, of 3000 tons, belonging to Howard, Smith & Co., I believe, the largest of the Inter-Colonial Steamers. After passing Wilson's Promontory, the extreme South point of Victoria, and indeed of Australia, the coast is in sight the whole way. After about 54 hours we entered Sydney Heads. It was then twilight, and quite dark before we came alongside the wharf.

The entrance to the Heads at Sydney is about a mile wide, but is scarcely seen before it is entered. The Cliffs on each side are several hundred feet high. The projecting points of the Cliff on the North side, when seen at a certain angle, made a good imitation of the Duke of Wellington's profile. A fast steamer from Melbourne takes about 48 hours, but then fast steamers are sometimes dangerous; most people have read of the terrible wrecks of the Cahers and the Lyeemoon, within a few months of each other, the two fastest steamers of the Australian Steam Navigation Co.; the latter wreck caused the loss of 70 lives. Both were the result of steering too close inland, to save an hour or two. To suspend or cancel a captain's certificate, or even to prosecute him, is a small consolation for such things as these. Moreover, when there is time to use the boats, they are too often found to be unseaworthy. The steamers themselves are inspected by the Marine Board, and certificates granted for 6 months, but the boats, though included in the certificate, are not separately examined. Being exposed to the hot sun day after day, they become very dry, and consequently leak when wanted for use. If the captain was bound to keep the boats seaworthy as distinct from the ship, he would be more careful to have them tested now and then. Mr. Wm. Smith, of Sydney, has recently invented a life-boat, which, it has been proved, cannot be upset. He has offered it freely to the Government, but owing to differences with some officials of the Marine Board, it has never received a fair trial at their hands. The recent loss of life at sea will not have been entirely useless, if it directs public attention to his most valuable invention. The harbour of Sydney has been often described, and I will not attempt to do so, especially as all descriptions of scenery are unsatisfactory. They seldom convey any definite impression, and a good photograph is better than any number of them. However, it disputes with that of Rio Janeiro, the name of the "finest harbour in the world"—whatever that may mean exactly. In shape it somewhat resembles a huge octopus, the innumerable creeks and inlets branching out like so many feelers, yet there can scarcely be said to be a centre from which they radiate. Numberless steamers ply all day to various points, mostly starting from the "Circular Quay," the principal wharf of the city. Small steamers rush in everywhere up the smallest rivers, and have to be of the lightest draught. In the summer many of the rivers are dry. The captain of one, not to be outbid by his rival, advertised to start "the next heavy dew."

I spent many of my days in Sydney in exploring the harbour, by the aid of steamers, but to see it adequately would require many weeks. Watson's Bay is near the South Head. Close by is the "Gap," where the City of Dunbar was wrecked on the 20th August, 1857. The anniversary of the day is kept. The Captain, steering straight for the entrance as he thought, ran upon the rocks. There was only one survivor, who was thrown upon a ledge of rock, and was not found for two days.

The ship was full of colonists returning home, and the calamity threw nearly all Sydney into mourning. There is now a light-house near at hand, with a magnificent electric light, which can be seen thirty miles away. At Manly Beach, near the North Head, is a fine sandy tract; it is a favourite bathing-place, and round about are many pretty villas. A young clergyman, recently come from England as *locum tenens* to an absent vicar, was then at Manly Beach with his wife. I had known him in England, so we made up a pic-nic to drive northward from Manly about 15 miles, to a place called Pitwater. A charming drive it was. Now and then glimpses of the sea on the right hand were seen. For several miles the road was bordered with the lovely wild flowers which grow in profusion near Sydney, so much so that in September the ladies of Manly get up a wild-flower show. The varieties of the wattle are especially beautiful. Pitwater consisted of one house, to which the road had been made but a few months previously. It was at the edge of an inlet from the sea, which here comes in some distance, but it looked like an inland lake, so still and solemn were the surroundings. My friend had the reputation of being one of the best, if not the best, preachers in Sydney. He occupied one of the largest churches and kept it full. His matter was excellent, but his reputation he owed chiefly to his admirable elocution, in which art he had taken lessons in London. If only more clergymen would have the sense to do the same! It is very well to say that, as religion is so

all-important a subject, any sermon should compel attention.
Perhaps that should be so, but men are mortal, and sermons
are not listened to any more than any other utterances if
they are tedious and badly delivered.

The area of New South Wales is over 300,000 square
miles, or half as large again as that of France. Its population
is a little under a million. Sydney, with 220,000, is the only
large town; there is not another above 15,000. There is
little agriculture and no manufactures to speak of. At Newcastle, about 60 miles north of Sydney, coal is found in abund-
ance, and from there most of Australia is supplied, but much
of it is of a dirty and smoky kind, more fit for steamers than for
domestic use. Coal has now been found in Gippsland, in
Victoria, and it is a question of carriage to bring it into use at
Melbourne. The New South Wales coal is about 21s. a ton
in Melbourne. The pastoral interest (sheep farming) is the
principal, almost the only interest in New South Wales, therefore when one drought follows another the whole colony is
of course depressed. At these times the public offices in
Sydney are besieged by crowds of men out of work, and the
Government will employ as many as possible, sometimes use-
lessly. This is a dangerous thing, for men speedily acquire the
notion that if they do nothing for themselves the Government
is bound to provide for them. But a man out of work in Sydney
or Melbourne is a different animal from the same man in
England. If offered 4s. 6d. a day for stone breaking he will

object that it blisters his hands. He wants not merely work, but work that he happens to like, and any politician who will provide him with work of this kind will be sure of his vote at the next election.

It is difficult to get at the truth about the state of the labour market in New South Wales. The newspaper accounts are most conflicting. One writer asserts that any man with honesty and determination can make his living at any time; another speaks of the numbers of skilled artisans who cannot get employment. But if some of these latter have the fastidious tastes above mentioned, it will be seen that the destitution is to a certain extent artificial. But reasoning on these subjects speedily merges in the ocean of Free Trade *v.* Protection, upon which I will not further touch. Sydney is the oldest town in the Colonies, having been founded in 1788. It has quite the air of an old established place—the abode of men for generations. The principal streets run East and West the whole length of the town down to the harbour, a distance of nearly four miles. In the centre is Hyde Park, a prettily laid-out piece of 40 acres, but the most beautiful spot is the Botanical Gardens, which slope down to the water's edge. Especial pains have been taken to render them an admirable specimen of horticulture. Nearly every tree and shrub that will grow in this climate is here to be found. Near them is the "National Gallery," where may be seen many paintings that a few years ago graced the walls of Burlington House. The chief attrac-

M

tion during my visit was a copy of Miss Thompson's, "Roll Call," said to be by the artist herself. £4000 was to be given for it on proof of its authenticity, but it did not require the eye of a connoisseur to judge that such proof was not likely to be forthcoming, and so it proved. It is evidently an inferior copy by another hand. The principal residential street is Macquarie Street, which faces the public gardens. Six years ago an Exhibition was held in these gardens. The building was mysteriously burned down, no doubt by incendiarism, but it was never found out, though it was jokingly said it was the act of some inhabitant of Macquarie Street, for the building quite obstructed their view.

I have before said that rents in Melbourne are very high. In Sydney they are much higher. The small house in which I boarded in Macquarie Street was rented at £5 10s. a week, and the landlord refused to make any repairs whatever, because, as he said, and truly enough, he could any day get £6 a week. In a London suburb the rent would be about £60 a year. Of course it was in the best situation in Sydney. In the outskirts of the town there was much land speculation. Land is sold at so much a foot, *i.e.* a strip of a foot in breadth, and about 360 feet in length. There is in Sydney a complete system of steam tramways, which run to the distance of six or seven miles out of the town. Accidents to pedestrians are not uncommon. Vehicles are hardly seen in the streets where the trams run. One line goes out as far as Botany. I walked from there along the famous bay which was so nearly having Sydney built upon its shore. It lies about seven miles North of Sydney, and is almost as quiet as when Captain Phillip landed a hundred years ago.

In New South Wales there are two Houses of Parliament and a Governor, as usual. The Lower House is elected by universal suffrage, but the Legislative Council is nominated by the Governor. The late Governor was certainly not popular, in spite of what the guide books say. Whether rightly or wrongly, there was a wide-spread impression that, being a comparatively poor man he had been sent out, like a Roman proconsul, to increase his private means. It is certain that a Governor of New South Wales cannot adequately discharge his numerous functions on less than his official salary of £7000 per annum, and any appearance of parsimony is naturally resented. It is not exactly the most suitable post for an elderly diplomatist accustomed to the pomps and inanities of European courts. The Attorney General of New South Wales, Mr. (now, I think, Sir William) Dalley, is by many people considered the foremost statesman in Australia. It was he, who, during the illness of the then Premier, despatched the contingent to the Soudan. He is, undoubtedly, a remarkable speaker, and has recently been created a Privy Councillor—the only colonial statesman hitherto raised to that dignity.

The Church of England flourishes in Sydney. There is the Cathedral of St. Andrew, and many other churches. The

Bishop (who is the Metropolitan of Australia), Dr. Barry, the late well-known principal of King's College, has done much by his broadness of view and liberality of sentiment to lessen local religious differences. The Roman Catholics have been building an enormous Cathedral, not yet finished. They, too, are a numerous body. The memory of the late Archbishop Vaughan, who died here in harness, is perfectly idolized by them. The University of Sydney has an imposing building, on a site over-looking the City, with a large hall and spacious lecture rooms. The late Professor of Classics was Dr. Badham, the renowned Greek scholar. The affiliated colleges are denominational, St. Paul's, Church of England; St. John's, Roman Catholic; and St. Andrew's, Presbyterian. There is, of course, a public library in Sydney, but it cannot for a moment compete with that of Melbourne, and, from a casual inspection, it did not appear to me that the books were well selected. There is also a public lending library. In Sydney there are a good many Chinese. Some of them are doctors. One Chinese doctor professes to make a diagnosis of any disease by mere inspection, and will then prescribe medicine to effect a cure in a week, a month, or a year, according to the patient's wish, the less the time the higher the price of the specific. I have heard that in China people pay their doctors as long as they are in good health, but when ill require their services for nothing. This appears a plan worth trying elsewhere. Unfortunately I did not have an opportunity of seeing more of New South Wales than Sydney and its immediate neighbourhood. One of the favourite excursions from Sydney, is to go by rail to Mount Victoria, about 80 miles, to pass over the celebrated "Zig-zag," a specimen of engineering skill, where the train climbs the mountain side, and at one point is so many hundred feet exactly above a point it passed some time before. To judge by a photograph it must resemble the line over the Brenner Pass in the Tyrol, where, near the station of Gossensass, there is a similar zig-zag.

Some large stalactite caverns, called the "Fish River Caves," are well worth a visit. Hitherto they have been nearly inaccessible to the ordinary tourist, but lately the Government has appointed a man to reside there, and the road has been made more practicable. From Sydney I returned by rail to Melbourne. The distance is nearly 600 miles, and the train takes 18 hours including stoppages, so that a very good speed is maintained all the way. At the frontier, which is reached about 6 a m., the traveller must change trains, as the gauge is wider in Victoria than on the New South Wales lines. After entering Victoria, the line passes through what is called the "Kelly Country," where the famous bushrangers, Kelly and his associates, committed their outrages some years ago. In a very short time Sydney will be connected by rail with Brisbane, and there will then be a continuous line from Adelaide through Melbourne and Sydney to Brisbane, a distance of not less than 1,600 miles. This will no doubt much increase the importance of Adelaide, because many people will be glad to land from a steamer as soon as possible. A few days after arrival at Melbourne, I returned by P. and O. steamer to England, and as I am not prepared to inflict on any one an account of so hackneyed a voyage, I finish at this point.

In ancient times colonists were sent out by Phœnicians or Greeks (the Roman colonies were for military and political purposes) among people who to them were barbarians (which, after all, only means people speaking a foreign tongue) but who might be only a little inferior to themselves in civilization. A Greek colony, for instance, settled among the Egyptians, by whom the Greeks themselves were accounted barbarians. The colonists to America from England two and a half centuries ago, had to contend with somewhat similar difficulties as the first colonists of Australia, but they had not so many modern appliances. The Australian Colonies are particularly interesting, because they exhibit people of an ancient civilization and fixed customs thrown into contact with the elemental conditions of life. They had to start at the very beginning, and that, too, with an overplus of criminal population. Their success hitherto is a testimony to the inherent vitality and tenacity of the English race, and to sneer at them as if they were children, or to patronize them, is not merely bad taste, but shows an utter ignorance of the facts. In many things they have begun where we left off. They have had the advantage of our experience, and in many things we may profitably learn from them. For instance, when we hear much airy talk of the nationalization of the land in England and other equally fundamental questions for a country to have to consider, it would be well to study the problem in Australia, where the greatest landlord is the State. Amid the conflict of forces which make up the struggle of life, it is not much use talking about rights and duties until the actual forces at work are taken into calculation. Not at all that might makes right, as Carlyle is often misrepresented to have said (of which he pathetically complains), but right that in the long run makes might; and the best social results are obtained by looking from this point of view at the many difficulties of our present existence.

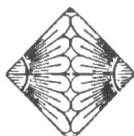

M. HARLAND & SON, Printers, Phœnix Works, Manor Street, Hull.

www.ingramcontent.com/pod-product-compliance
Lightning Source LLC
Chambersburg PA
CBHW032246080426
42735CB00008B/1028

* 9 7 8 3 3 3 7 1 0 9 4 3 1 *